ECONOMIC ISSUES, PROBLEMS AND PERSPECTIVES

FEDERAL RULEMAKING

OVERVIEW AND THE USE OF COST-BENEFIT ANALYSIS IN SIGNIFICANT RULES

Economic Issues, Problems and Perspectives

Additional books in this series can be found on Nova's website under the Series tab.

Additional e-books in this series can be found on Nova's website under the e-book tab.

ECONOMIC ISSUES, PROBLEMS AND PERSPECTIVES

FEDERAL RULEMAKING

OVERVIEW AND THE USE OF COST-BENEFIT ANALYSIS IN SIGNIFICANT RULES

NORMAN A. ELWIN
EDITOR

nova publishers
New York

Library of Congress Cataloging-in-Publication Data

ISSN: 1549-1552

ISBN: 978-1-63463-724-4

Published by Nova Science Publishers, Inc. † New York

CONTENTS

PREFACE

This book addresses how often and to what extent significant, economically significant, and major rules include key elements for assessing or analyzing benefits and costs; and how and to what extent agencies assess the quality of the scientific, technical, and other types of data they use to consider benefits and costs. The purpose of this book is to provide Congress with an overview of the federal rulemaking process and a brief discussion of the major laws and executive orders that prescribe the procedures agencies are to apply when promulgating regulations.

Chapter 1 – Federal regulation, like taxing and spending, is one of the basic tools of government used to implement public policy. Although not as frequently examined as congressional or presidential policy making, the process of developing and framing rules is viewed by some as central to the definition and implementation of public policy in the United States.

Regulations generally start with an act of Congress, and are the means by which statutes are implemented and specific requirements are established. The terms “rule” or “regulation” are often used interchangeably in discussions of the federal regulatory process. The Administrative Procedure Act of 1946 defines a *rule* as “the whole or part of an agency statement of general or particular applicability and future effect designed to implement, interpret, or prescribe law or policy.” The procedures that federal agencies are required to follow in writing regulations are called the rulemaking process, and are the subject of this report.

During the past 60 to 70 years, Congress and various Presidents have developed an elaborate set of procedures and requirements to guide the federal rulemaking process. Statutory rulemaking requirements applicable to a wide range of agencies include the Administrative Procedure Act, the Regulatory

Flexibility Act, the Paperwork Reduction Act, the Unfunded Mandates Reform Act, and the Information Quality Act. These and other cross-cutting rulemaking requirements often require some type of analysis on the part of the rulemaking agency before issuing a covered rule, but also often give agencies substantial discretion regarding whether the requirements are applicable. Other statutorily based rulemaking requirements are contained in agency- or program-specific laws, which provide varying levels of discretion regarding the substance of agencies' rules and may impose (or exclude) additional analytical or procedural requirements.

In addition to statutory requirements, Presidents have also imposed their own requirements on federal agencies when issuing rules. The most important of the current set of presidential rulemaking requirements are in Executive Order 12866, which establishes presidential review of covered agencies' rulemaking within the Office of Management and Budget's (OMB's) Office of Information and Regulatory Affairs (OIRA). The executive order requires covered agencies to submit their significant rules to OIRA for review before they become final, and requires those rules to meet certain minimal standards. Other executive orders and presidential directives delineate other specific rulemaking requirements incumbent on covered agencies. However, these requirements also often provide substantial discretion to agencies regarding whether, and if so how, they are applied.

The purpose of this report is to provide Congress with an overview of the federal rulemaking process and a brief discussion of the major laws and executive orders that prescribe the procedures agencies are to apply when promulgating regulations.

Chapter 2 – Federal agencies issue thousands of regulations each year to achieve national goals. For the few hundred of these rules deemed to be significant, agencies are required to assess expected costs and benefits. For the subset of these rules estimated to have the greatest economic impact, agencies must also include an assessment of alternatives.

GAO was asked to review agencies' compliance with broadly applicable directives and guidance related to significant federal rulemaking. This report addresses (1) how often and to what extent significant, economically significant, and major rules include key elements for assessing or analyzing benefits and costs; and (2) how and to what extent agencies assess the quality of the scientific, technical, and other types of data they use to consider benefits and costs. To answer these objectives, GAO reviewed a generalizable sample of 109 significant and 57 economically significant rules issued by executive agencies and all 37 major rules issued by independent agencies and published in the *Federal Register* from July 1, 2011, to June 30, 2013. GAO also conducted roundtable discussions with the 17 executive and independent agencies with the largest number of rules in GAO's sample.

In: Federal Rulemaking
Editor: Norman A. Elwin
ISBN: 978-1-63463-724-4

Chapter 1

THE FEDERAL RULEMAKING PROCESS: AN OVERVIEW*

Maeve P. Carey

SUMMARY

Federal regulation, like taxing and spending, is one of the basic tools of government used to implement public policy. Although not as frequently examined as congressional or presidential policy making, the process of developing and framing rules is viewed by some as central to the definition and implementation of public policy in the United States.

Regulations generally start with an act of Congress, and are the means by which statutes are implemented and specific requirements are established. The terms "rule" or "regulation" are often used interchangeably in discussions of the federal regulatory process. The Administrative Procedure Act of 1946 defines a *rule* as "the whole or part of an agency statement of general or particular applicability and future effect designed to implement, interpret, or prescribe law or policy." The procedures that federal agencies are required to follow in writing regulations are called the rulemaking process, and are the subject of this report.

During the past 60 to 70 years, Congress and various Presidents have developed an elaborate set of procedures and requirements to guide the

---

* This is an edited, reformatted and augmented version of a Congressional Research Service publication RL32240, prepared for Members and Committees of Congress, dated June 17, 2013.

federal rulemaking process. Statutory rulemaking requirements applicable to a wide range of agencies include the Administrative Procedure Act, the Regulatory Flexibility Act, the Paperwork Reduction Act, the Unfunded Mandates Reform Act, and the Information Quality Act. These and other cross-cutting rulemaking requirements often require some type of analysis on the part of the rulemaking agency before issuing a covered rule, but also often give agencies substantial discretion regarding whether the requirements are applicable. Other statutorily based rulemaking requirements are contained in agency- or program-specific laws, which provide varying levels of discretion regarding the substance of agencies' rules and may impose (or exclude) additional analytical or procedural requirements.

In addition to statutory requirements, Presidents have also imposed their own requirements on federal agencies when issuing rules. The most important of the current set of presidential rulemaking requirements are in Executive Order 12866, which establishes presidential review of covered agencies' rulemaking within the Office of Management and Budget's (OMB's) Office of Information and Regulatory Affairs (OIRA). The executive order requires covered agencies to submit their significant rules to OIRA for review before they become final, and requires those rules to meet certain minimal standards. Other executive orders and presidential directives delineate other specific rulemaking requirements incumbent on covered agencies. However, these requirements also often provide substantial discretion to agencies regarding whether, and if so how, they are applied.

The purpose of this report is to provide Congress with an overview of the federal rulemaking process and a brief discussion of the major laws and executive orders that prescribe the procedures agencies are to apply when promulgating regulations.

INTRODUCTION

Federal regulation, like taxing and spending, is one of the basic tools of government used to implement public policy. In fact, the development and framing of a rule has been described as "the climactic act of the policy making process."[1] Another observer described the rulemaking process as "a ubiquitous presence in virtually all government programs.... The crucial intermediate process of rulemaking stands between the enactment of a law by Congress and the realization of the goals that both Congress and the people it represents seek to achieve by that law."[2] Regulations generally start with an act of Congress, and are one of the means through which statutes are implemented and specific requirements are established. Federal agencies usually issue more than 3,000 final rules each year on topics ranging from the timing of bridge openings to the permissible levels of arsenic and other contaminants in drinking water. The costs and benefits associated with all federal regulations have been a subject of great controversy, with the costs estimated in the hundreds of billions of dollars and the benefits estimates generally even higher.

The terms "rule" or "regulation" are often used interchangeably in discussions of the federal regulatory process. The Administrative Procedure Act (APA) of 1946 defines a rule as "the whole or part of an agency statement of general or particular applicability and future effect designed to implement, interpret, or prescribe law or policy."[3] The process by which federal agencies develop, amend, or repeal rules is called "rulemaking," and is the subject of this report.

Figure 1 illustrates the basic process that most federal agencies are generally required to follow in writing or revising a significant rule. However, some aspects of *Figure 1* do not apply to all rules. For example, as discussed later in this report, an agency may, in certain circumstances, issue a final rule without issuing a notice of proposed rulemaking, thereby skipping several steps depicted in the figure. On the other hand, some rules may be published for public comment more than once. Also, independent regulatory agencies are not required to submit their rules to the Office of Management and Budget's (OMB) Office of Information and Regulatory Affairs (OIRA) for review, and no agency is required to do so for rules that are not "significant."[4]

Note at the top of *Figure 1* that the rulemaking process begins when Congress passes a statute either requiring or authorizing an agency to write and issue certain types of regulations. An initiating event (e.g., a recommendation from an outside body or a catastrophic accident) can prompt either legislation or regulation (where regulatory action has already been authorized). For example, in response to lethal chemical releases by plants in Bhopal, India, and West Virginia, Congress enacted Section 313 of the Emergency Planning and Community Right-to-Know Act of 1986 (42 U.S.C. §§11001-11050, 11023). The act required the owners and operators of certain types of facilities to report the amounts of various toxic chemicals that the facilities release to the environment above certain thresholds, and it requires the Environmental Protection Agency (EPA) to make this information available to the public. EPA subsequently issued detailed regulations implementing these requirements and, using the authority provided to it through the statute, has required reporting for more than 300 toxic substances in addition to those delineated in the law.

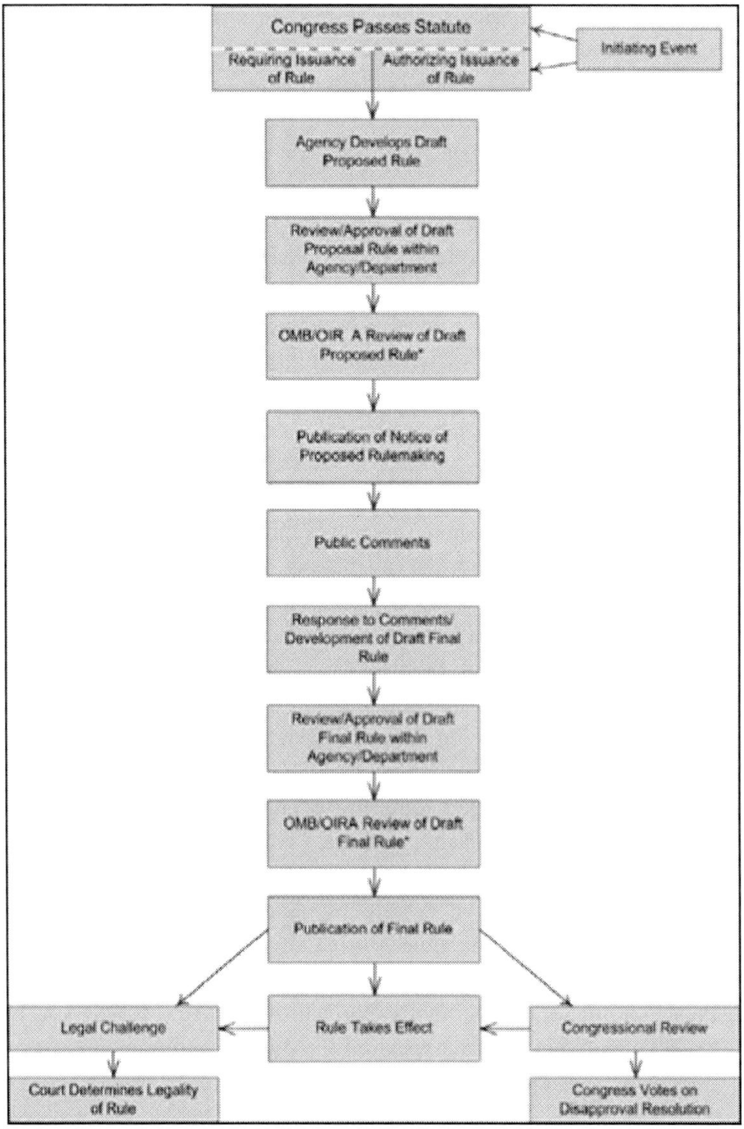

Source: CRS.

* The Office of Management and Budget's (OMB) office of Information and Regulatory Affairs (OIRA) reviews only significant rules, and does not review any rules submitted by independent regulatory agencies.

Figure 1. Federal Rulemaking Process.

As this example illustrates, the authority to regulate rests with Congress and is delegated, through law, to an agency. The statutory basis for a regulation can vary greatly in terms of its specificity, from (1) very broad grants of authority that state only the general intent of the legislation and leave agencies with a great deal of discretion as to how that intent should be implemented, to (2) very specific requirements delineating exactly what regulatory agencies should do and how they should take action. Note also in *Figure 1* the roles that Congress and the courts can play at the end of the rulemaking process, which may result in a rule being returned to an earlier point in the process or being vacated by the reviewing body. Congress may also play a role at other stages in the process through its oversight and appropriations responsibilities.

Implicit within the steps depicted in *Figure 1* is an elaborate set of procedures and requirements that Congress and various Presidents have developed during the past 60 to 70 years to guide the federal rulemaking process. Some of these rulemaking requirements apply to virtually all federal agencies, some apply only to certain types of agencies, and others are agency-specific. Collectively, these rulemaking provisions are voluminous and require a wide range of procedural, consultative, and analytical actions on the part of rulemaking agencies. Some observers contend that the requirements have resulted in the "ossification" of the rulemaking process, causing agencies to take years to develop final rules.[5] For example, the National Advisory Committee on Occupational Safety and Health noted that it takes the Occupational Safety and Health Administration (OSHA) within the Department of Labor an average of 10 years to develop and promulgate a health or safety standard.[6] On the other hand, while these congressional and presidential rulemaking requirements are numerous, it is not clear whether they or some other factors (e.g., lack of data, congressionally imposed delays, court challenges, etc.) are the primary cause of the long time-frames that are sometimes required to develop and publish final rules.

STATUTORY RULEMAKING REQUIREMENTS

Statutory rulemaking requirements can be generally categorized into two groups—those that are specific to an individual agency or program and those that are more cross-cutting in nature and therefore apply to a wider range of agencies or programs. Agency- or program-specific rulemaking requirements may be in authorizing or appropriating statutes, and can have a significant or even determinative effect on an agency's rules and rulemaking procedures. As noted previously, these statutes sometimes specifically delineate what the agency's rules should require. For example, the Employee Retirement Income Security Act (29 U.S.C. §1001 *et seq.*) gives the Pension Benefit Guaranty Corporation no discretion in drafting rules that establish minimum pension insurance premium rates, specifying to the dollar what those rates should be.[7] Also, for a number of years the Department of Transportation (DOT) concluded that it had no discretion in setting the average fuel economy standards for light trucks, and was required to keep the standard at 20.7 miles per gallon.[8] Agency-specific statutes may also impose specific procedural requirements on their rulemaking processes (e.g., the conduct of public hearings, the publication of a notice of proposed rulemaking by a particular date, or the coordination of rulemaking with another agency).

In other cases, however, statutes may give rulemaking agencies substantial discretion in how rules are developed and what they require. For example, the Agricultural Adjustment Act provides a broad grant of rulemaking authority to the Secretary of Agriculture, stating only that agricultural marketing should be "orderly" but providing little guidance regarding which crops should have marketing orders or how to apportion the market among growers.[9] More recently, the Patient Protection and Affordable Care Act (ACA, P.L. 111-148) contained a number of provisions giving federal agencies broad authority to issue "such regulations as may be necessary" to carry out certain requirements in the law.[10]

Agency rulemaking is also often significantly influenced by court decisions interpreting these agency- or program-specific statutory requirements. For example, in 1980, the Supreme Court ruled that, before promulgating new health standards, OSHA must demonstrate that the particular chemical to be regulated poses a "significant risk" under workplace conditions permitted by current regulations.[11] The court also said that OSHA must demonstrate that the new limit OSHA proposes will substantially reduce that risk. This decision effectively requires OSHA to evaluate the risks associated with exposure to a chemical and to determine that these risks are "significant" before issuing a regulatory standard. Other court decisions have required OSHA rulemaking to demonstrate the technical and economic feasibility of its requirements.[12] Still other decisions have required agencies to permit meaningful public participation in rulemaking and to fully explain what they considered and why they did and did not take particular actions.[13]

The following discussion of statutory rulemaking requirements focuses solely on the cross-cutting requirements that are applicable to more than one agency. The discussion provides descriptions of some of the major rulemaking-related statutes and is not intended to be a catalogue of all such requirements. Some of these rulemaking requirements have been in place for more than 70 years, but most have been implemented within the past 30 years. Some of these statutory requirements apply to Cabinet departments and independent agencies; others apply to those agencies as well as the independent regulatory agencies.

Federal Register Act

With the surge of New Deal legislation enacted in the 1930s, Congress made federal agencies responsible for issuing detailed regulations on a variety of complex social and economic issues. However, no central regulatory publication system existed, so there was no efficient way for citizens to know about regulations that affected them. Therefore, Congress enacted the Federal Register Act, which became law in July 1935 (44 U.S.C. Chapter 15). The act established a uniform system for handling agency regulations by requiring (1) the filing of documents with the Office of the Federal Register, (2) the placement of documents on public inspection, (3) publication of the documents in the *Federal Register*, and (4) (after a 1937 amendment) permanent codification of rules in the *Code of Federal Regulations*. Publication of a rule in the *Federal Register* provides official notice of its existence and contents. Other documents that are generally published in the *Federal Register* include presidential proclamations and executive orders, notices, and documents that the President or Congress requires to be published.

Regulations for carrying out the Federal Register Act deal with, among other things, the format and distribution of the *Federal Register* and how documents are prepared, transmitted, and processed.[14] The Office of the Federal Register is responsible for printing and distributing the *Federal Register*, and the Office has published a guide and a drafting handbook explaining how *Federal Register* documents are to be prepared. The *Federal Register* is published each business day, and is now available electronically.[15]

Administrative Procedure Act

The most long-standing and broadly applicable federal rulemaking requirements are in the Administrative Procedure Act (APA) of 1946 (5 U.S.C. §551 *et seq.*). The APA was written to bring regularity and predictability to agency decisionmaking, and it provides for both formal and informal rulemaking. Formal rulemaking is used in ratemaking proceedings and in certain other cases when rules are required by statute to be made "on the record" after an opportunity for a trial-type agency hearing.[16] However, few statutes require such on-the-record hearings. Informal rulemaking, also known as "notice and comment" rulemaking, is used much more frequently, and is the focus of this section.[17]

In informal rulemaking, the APA generally requires that agencies (Cabinet departments and independent agencies as well as independent regulatory agencies) publish a notice of proposed rulemaking (NPRM) in the *Federal Register*.[18] The notice must contain (1) a statement of the time, place, and nature of public rulemaking proceedings; (2) reference to the legal authority under which the rule is proposed; and (3) either the terms or substance of the proposed rule or a description of the subjects and issues involved. After giving "interested persons" an opportunity to comment on the proposed rule, and after considering the public comments, the agency may then publish the final rule, incorporating a general statement of its basis and purpose. Although the APA does not specify the length of this public comment period, agencies commonly allow at least 30 days.[19] Public comments as well as other supporting materials (e.g., hearing records or agency regulatory studies but generally not internal memoranda) are placed in a rulemaking "docket" which must be available for public inspection. Finally, the APA states that the final rule cannot become effective until at least 30 days after its publication unless (1) the rule grants or recognizes an exemption or relieves a restriction, (2) the rule is an interpretative rule or a statement of policy, or (3) the agency determines that the rule should take effect sooner for good cause, and publishes that determination with the rule.

The final rule cannot adopt a provision if the NPRM did not clearly provide notice to the public that the agency was considering adopting it. If challenged in court under the APA, an agency rulemaking can be held unlawful or set aside if it is found to be "arbitrary, capricious, an abuse of discretion, or otherwise not in accordance with the law."[20] The court can also "compel agency action unlawfully withheld or unreasonably delayed."

Amendment or revocation of an existing rule generally requires the responsible agency to issue a new rule through the APA process.

Exceptions to the APA Notice Requirement

Although the APA generally requires agencies to publish NPRMs before promulgating a final rule, the act provides exceptions to this requirement. For example, the APA states that the notice and comment procedures generally do not apply when an agency finds, for "good cause," that those procedures are "impracticable, unnecessary, or contrary to the public interest." When agencies use the good cause exception, the act requires that they explicitly say so and provide a rationale for the exception's use when the rule is published in the *Federal Register*. The APA also provides explicit exceptions to the NPRM requirement for certain categories of regulatory actions, such as rules dealing with military or foreign affairs; agency management or personnel; or public property, loans, grants, benefits, or contracts. Further, the APA says that the NPRM requirements do not apply to interpretative rules; general statements of policy; or rules of agency organization, procedure, or practice.[21] However, these rules do have to be published in the *Federal Register*.

The legislative history of the APA makes it clear that Congress did not believe that the act's good cause exception to the notice and comment requirements should be an "escape clause." According to the Senate committee's report accompanying the APA, a "true and supported or supportable finding of necessity or emergency must be made and published" when the agency uses the good cause exception.[22] The legislative history also indicates that Congress envisioned agencies using the notice and comment procedures even in some cases in which the APA's exceptions applied.

A federal agency's invocation of the good cause exception (or other exceptions to notice and comment procedures) is subject to judicial review. After having reviewed the totality of circumstances, the courts can and sometimes do determine that an agency's reliance on the good cause exception was not authorized under the APA.[23] The case law has generally reinforced the view that the good cause exception should be "narrowly construed."[24]

Two procedures for noncontroversial and expedited rulemaking were designed not to involve NPRMs. "Direct final" rulemaking involves agency publication of a rule in the *Federal Register* with a statement that the rule will be effective on a particular date unless an adverse comment is received within a specified period of time (e.g., 30 days). However, if an adverse comment is filed, the "direct final rule" is withdrawn and the agency may publish the rule as a proposed rule under normal NPRM procedures. "Direct final" rulemaking can be viewed as a particular application of the APA's good cause exception in which agencies claim NPRMs are "unnecessary."[25] Both Vice President Albert Gore's National Performance Review and the Administrative Conference of the United States encouraged agencies to use direct final rulemaking for noncontroversial rules.[26]

The Administrative Conference also endorsed the use of what is known as "interim final" rulemaking, in which an agency issues a final rule without an NPRM that is generally effective immediately, but with a post-promulgation opportunity for the public to comment. If the public comments persuade the agency that changes are needed in the "interim final" rule, the agency may revise the rule by publishing a final rule reflecting those changes. "Interim final" rulemaking can be viewed as another particular application of the good cause exception in the APA, but with the addition of a comment period after the rule has become effective.[27]

Congress sometimes requires agencies to use "interim final" rulemaking, and may also specify the length of the comment period. For example, Subsection (b)(2) of Section 1104 of the Patient Protection and Affordable Care Act amended Section 1173 of the Social Security Act (at 42 U.S.C. §1320d-2) and states, in part, that the Secretary "shall promulgate an interim final rule applying any standard or operating rule recommended by the National Committee on Vital and Health Statistics," and "shall accept and consider public comments on any interim final rule published under this subparagraph for 60 days after the date of such publication."

In August 1998, the General Accounting Office (GAO, now the Government Accountability Office) reported that about half of the 4,658 final regulatory actions published in the *Federal Register* during 1997 were published without NPRMs.[28] Seven agencies accounted for about 70% of both the final actions and the actions without NPRMs. Most of the actions without NPRMs appeared to involve administrative or technical issues with limited applicability. However, 11 of the 61 final rules published during 1997 that were "major" (e.g., having a $100 million impact on the economy) did not have NPRMs. The agencies most commonly cited the APA's good cause exception as their justification for not publishing NPRMs, frequently noting the time-sensitive nature of the actions being taken. The agencies also frequently used the categorical exceptions permitted in the APA (e.g., actions involving agencies' management or personnel). In some cases GAO concluded that the agencies' explanations for why NPRMs were not used were not clear or understandable, with the agencies sometimes making broad assertions that an NPRM would delay the issuance of rules that were, in some general sense, in the public interest. For example, in one case the agency said that soliciting public comments on the rule was "contrary to the public interest" because the rule authorized a "new and creative method of financing the development of public housing."[29]

National Environmental Policy Act

The National Environmental Policy Act (NEPA) of 1969 (42 U.S.C. §§4321-4347) was the first statute to require an "impact statement" as a way to ensure that federal agencies give special consideration to certain issues during the rulemaking process. NEPA requires all federal agencies to include in every recommendation or report related to "major Federal actions significantly affecting the quality of the human environment" a detailed statement on the environmental impact of the proposed action. Initially, though, agencies make a threshold determination (known as an "environmental assessment") as to whether the rule or other action represents a significant impact on the environment. If not, the agency issues a "finding of no significant impact." If the agency concludes that there is a significant impact, the agency then prepares a full "environmental impact statement" describing the likely effects of the rule.

According to the act and its implementing regulations developed by the Council on Environmental Quality (CEQ), the environmental impact statement must delineate the direct, indirect, and cumulative effects of the proposed action.[30] Agencies are also required to include in the statement (1) any adverse environmental effects that cannot be avoided should the proposal be implemented, (2) alternatives to the proposed action, (3) the relationship between local short-term uses of the environment and the maintenance and enhancement of long-term productivity, and (4) any irreversible and irretrievable commitments of resources that would be involved if the proposed action should be implemented. Before developing any such environmental impact statement, NEPA requires the responsible federal official to consult with and obtain comments of any federal agency that has jurisdiction by law or special expertise with respect to any environmental impact involved. Agencies must make copies of the statement and the comments and views of appropriate federal, state, and local agencies available to the President, the CEQ, and to the public. The adequacy of an agency's environmental impact statement is subject to judicial review.

In April 2002, the chairman of the CEQ established a task force composed of federal agency employees to review NEPA implementation practices and procedures. In September 2003, the task force issued a report containing more than 50 recommendations to expedite the NEPA review process.[31] Among other things, the task force recommended that new guidance be developed setting standards for the documentation needed to support a determination that a rule would not have significant environmental effects. Also, several pieces of legislation have been enacted since 2008 in an effort to streamline the NEPA process.[32]

Paperwork Reduction Act

The Paperwork Reduction Act (PRA) (44 U.S.C. §§3501-3520) was originally enacted in 1980. One of the purposes of the PRA is to minimize the paperwork burden for individuals, small businesses, and others resulting from the collection of information by or for the federal government. The act generally defines a "collection of information" as the obtaining or disclosure of facts or opinions by or for an agency by 10 or more nonfederal persons. Many information collections, recordkeeping requirements, and third-party disclosures are contained in or are authorized by regulations as monitoring or enforcement tools. In fact, these paperwork requirements are the essence of many agencies' regulatory provisions.[33] The PRA requires agencies to justify any collection of information from the public by establishing the need and intended use of the information, estimating the burden that the collection will impose on respondents, and showing that the collection is the least burdensome way to gather the information.

The original PRA established OIRA within OMB to provide central agency leadership and oversight of government-wide efforts to reduce unnecessary paperwork burden and improve the management of information resources. Agencies must receive OIRA approval (signified by an OMB control number displayed on the information collection) for each collection request before it is implemented, and those approvals must be renewed at least every three years. Failure to obtain OIRA approval for an active collection, or the lapse of that approval, represents a violation of the act, and triggers the PRA's public protection provision. Under that provision, no one can be penalized for failing to comply with a collection of information subject to the act if the collection does not display a valid OMB control number.[34] OIRA can disapprove any collection of information if it believes the collection is inconsistent with the requirements of the PRA.[35]

The PRA clearance process is described in the act and implementing regulations. For new collections, no later than the publication of the NPRM, the issuing agency must submit the proposed rule and any background information to OIRA. At the same time the agency is required to publish a notice in the *Federal Register* stating that OIRA's approval is being sought, thereby providing the public with an opportunity to comment on the proposed collection. For any collection of information that is not contained in a proposed rule, OIRA staff have up to 60 days under the statute to review the proposed collection and ensure, among other things, that the collection is statutorily authorized and necessary, and that the agency's paperwork burden estimate (most commonly measured in terms of "burden hours") is reasonable.[36] At the end of the process the agency is notified of the disposition of the review. OIRA data indicates that the office takes action on between 3,000 and 5,000 information collection requests (new approvals, renewals, or revisions) each year.

The PRA was amended in 1995. The amended version reaffirmed the principles in the original act and gave significant new responsibilities to OIRA and executive branch agencies. For example, the act currently requires OIRA to "oversee the use of information resources to improve the efficiency and effectiveness of governmental operations to serve agency missions." The PRA also requires federal agencies to establish a process, independent of program responsibility, to evaluate proposed collections of information, manage information resources to reduce information collection burdens on the public, and ensure that the public has timely and equitable access to information products and services.

The coverage of the PRA is extremely broad, including actions by both Cabinet departments and independent agencies as well as independent regulatory agencies, and covering virtually any type of collection of information that these agencies "conduct or sponsor."[37] As a result of the 1995 amendments to the act, the PRA's clearance requirements clearly cover collections of information "requiring the disclosure to third parties or the public," effectively overturning the Supreme Court's 1990 decision in *Dole v. United Steelworkers of America* (494 U.S. 26).

One of the key features of the PRA of 1995 was the requirement that OIRA, in consultation with the agency heads, set annual government-wide goals for the reduction of information collection burdens by at least 10% in fiscal years 1996 and 1997, and by at least 5% in each of the succeeding four fiscal years. The act also required OIRA to establish agency burden reduction goals each year representing "the maximum practicable opportunity in each agency." At the end of FY1995 (just before the PRA of 1995 took effect), federal agencies estimated that their information collections imposed about 7 billion burden hours on the public. Therefore, if all federal agencies had been able to meet each of the government-wide goals, by September 30, 2001, the burden-hour estimate would have decreased about 35% to about 4.6 billion hours. However, this reduction did not occur. In fact, the September 30, 2002, government-wide burden estimate stood at more than 8.2 billion hours—a 17% *increase* since the PRA of 1995 took effect. Nearly half of that increase occurred during FY2002 alone, and about 70% occurred during fiscal years 2001 and 2002.[38] The agencies contend that they are often unable to reduce paperwork requirements without changes in the underlying statutes that require the information to be collected.[39] As of January 2013, there were more than 9,000 active agency information collections, with a total burden-hour estimate of over 10 billion hours.[40]

Regulatory Flexibility Act

The Regulatory Flexibility Act (RFA) of 1980 (5 U.S.C. §§601-612), requires federal agencies to assess the impact of their forthcoming regulations on "small entities," which the act defines as including small businesses, small governmental jurisdictions, and certain small not-for-profit organizations. Under the RFA, Cabinet departments and independent agencies as well as independent regulatory agencies must prepare a regulatory flexibility analysis at the time certain proposed and final rules are issued. The analysis for a proposed rule is referred to as an "initial regulatory flexibility analysis" (IRFA) and the analysis for a final rule is referred to as a "final regulatory flexibility analysis." The RFA requires the analysis to describe, among other things, (1) the reasons why the regulatory action is being considered; (2) the small entities to which the proposed rule will apply and, where feasible, an estimate of their number; (3) the projected reporting, recordkeeping, and other compliance requirements of the proposed rule; and (4) any significant alternatives to the rule that would accomplish the statutory objectives while minimizing the impact on small entities.

However, these analytical requirements are not triggered if the head of the issuing agency certifies that the proposed rule would not have a "significant economic impact on a substantial number of small entities." The RFA does not define "significant economic impact" or "substantial number of small entities," thereby giving federal agencies substantial discretion regarding when the act's analytical requirements are initiated. Also, the RFA's analytical requirements do not apply to final rules for which the agency does not publish a proposed rule.[41]

The RFA initially did not permit judicial review of agencies' actions under the act. However, amendments to the act in 1996 as part of the Small Business Regulatory Enforcement Fairness Act (SBREFA) (110 Stat. 857, 5 U.S.C. §601 note) permitted judicial review regarding, among other things, agencies' regulatory flexibility analyses for final rules and any certifications that their rules will not have a significant impact on small entities. As a result, a small entity that is adversely affected or aggrieved by an agency's determination that its final rule would not have a significant impact on small entities could seek judicial review of that determination within one year of the date of the final agency action. In granting relief, a court may remand the rule to the agency or defer enforcement against small entities. The addition of judicial review in 1996 is generally viewed as a significant strengthening of the RFA, and is believed to have improved agencies' compliance with the act.[42]

The RFA also contains several other notable provisions. For example, Section 602 requires each federal agency to publish a "regulatory flexibility agenda" in the *Federal Register* each October and April listing regulations that the agency expects to propose or promulgate which are likely to have a significant economic impact on a substantial number of small entities.[43] Section 610 of the act requires agencies to review those rules that have or will have a significant impact within 10 years of their promulgation to determine whether they should be continued without change or should be amended or rescinded to minimize their impact on small entities. Section 612 of the RFA requires the Chief Counsel of the Small Business Administration's (SBA) Office of Advocacy to monitor and report at least annually on agencies' compliance with the act. SBA's primary method of monitoring agencies' compliance is to review and comment on proposed regulations when they are published for notice and comment in the *Federal Register*. However, the statute also specifically authorizes the Chief Counsel to appear as *amicus curiae* (i.e., "friend of the court") in any court action to review a rule.

The RFA also requires agencies to ensure that small entities have an opportunity to participate in the rulemaking process, and it has special requirements for proposed rules issued by the Environmental Protection Agency (EPA), the Occupational Safety and Health Administration (OSHA), and the Consumer Financial Protection Bureau (CFPB).[44] Specifically, these three agencies are required to convene "advocacy review panels" before publishing a regulatory flexibility analysis for a proposed rule. The agency issuing the regulation must notify the SBA Chief Counsel for Advocacy and provide information on the draft rule's potential impacts on small entities and the type of small entities that might be affected. The Chief Counsel then must identify representatives of affected small entities within 15 days of the notification. The review panel must consist of full-time federal employees from the rulemaking agency, the Office of Management and Budget, and SBA's Chief Counsel for Advocacy. During the panel process, the panel must collect the advice and recommendations of representatives of affected small entities about the potential impact of the draft rule. The panel must report on the comments received and on the panel's recommendations no later than 60 days after the panel is convened, and the panel's report must be made public as part of the rulemaking record.[45] The agency may or may not adopt the panel's recommendations.

GAO has examined the implementation of the RFA several times within the past 20 years, and a recurring theme in GAO's reports is a lack of clarity in the act and a resulting variability in the act's implementation. For example, in 1991 GAO reported that each of the four federal agencies that it reviewed had a different interpretation of key RFA provisions.[46] In 1994 GAO again reported that agencies' compliance with the RFA varied widely from one agency to another and that agencies were interpreting the statute differently.[47] In a 1999 report on the implementation of Section 610 of the RFA and in a 2000 report on the implementation of the RFA at the Environmental Protection Agency (EPA), GAO concluded that agencies had broad discretion to determine what the statute required.[48] In all of these reports, GAO suggested that Congress consider clarifying the act's requirements and/or give SBA or some other entity the responsibility to develop criteria for whether and how agencies should conduct RFA analyses. In 2001, GAO testified that the promise of the RFA may never be realized until Congress or some other entity defines what a "significant economic impact" and a "substantial number of small entities" mean in a rulemaking setting.[49] However, other observers have indicated that the definitions of these terms should remain flexible because of significant differences in each agency's operating environment.

Periodically, legislation is introduced to amend the RFA. For example, in the 112th Congress, H.R. 527, the Regulatory Flexibility Improvements Act of 2011, would (among other things) clarify and expand the rules covered by the act, and require the SBA Chief Counsel for Advocacy to "issue rules governing agency compliance with this chapter."[50]

Small Business Regulatory Enforcement Fairness Act

As noted in the previous section of this report, certain provisions in SBREFA amended the RFA to permit judicial review and to permit small entities to participate in EPA and OSHA rulemaking before a proposed rule with a significant impact on small entities is published. Other provisions in SBREFA did not amend the RFA, but imposed new rulemaking-related requirements on federal agencies.

For example, Section 212 of SBREFA requires agencies to develop one or more compliance guides for each final rule or group of related final rules for which the agency is required to prepare a regulatory flexibility analysis. Specifically, Section 212 requires the guides to (1) be published, (2) be designated as "small entity compliance guides," and (3) explain the actions a small entity is required to take to comply with an associated final rule. However, the discretion inherent in the RFA regarding when a regulatory flexibility analysis is required also applies to whether compliance guides must be developed. Section 212 gives agencies broad discretion in other areas as well. For example, it says agencies "may" prepare separate guides covering groups or classes of similarly affected small entities, and "may" cooperate with associations of small entities to develop and distribute the guides. Agencies are given "sole discretion" in the use of plain language in the guides. The statute does not indicate when the guides must be developed or how they must be "published." In December 2001, GAO reported that Section 212 of SBREFA did not appear to have had much of an impact on agencies' rulemaking activities, and its implementation varied across and sometimes within agencies.[51] Using the discretion that the section provided, GAO said "an agency could legally exclude all of its rules from coverage by the statute, designate a previously published document as its small entity compliance guide, or develop and publish a guide with no input from small entities years after the covered rule takes effect." GAO recommended several changes it felt were needed to strengthen and clarify the requirements in Section 212.[52]

Section 213 of SBREFA required federal agencies regulating the activities of small entities to establish a program for responding to inquiries concerning compliance with applicable statutes and regulations. The section also says that in any civil or administrative action against a small entity, such guidance "may be considered as evidence of the reasonableness or appropriateness of any proposed fines, penalties or damages sought against such small entity."

Section 222 of SBREFA amended the Small Business Act (15 U.S.C. §631 *et seq.*) to require the SBA Administrator to designate a "Small Business and Agriculture Regulatory Enforcement Ombudsman," who was directed to work with each agency to ensure that small business concerns have an opportunity to comment on agencies' enforcement actions. The ombudsman was directed to annually evaluate and report on each agency's enforcement activities, including a rating of the "responsiveness to small business" of each agency's regional and program offices. Section 222 also required the Administrator to establish a "Small Business Regulatory Fairness Board" in each SBA regional office to report to and advise the ombudsman on "excessive enforcement actions of agencies against small business concerns."

Section 223 of SBREFA requires agencies to provide small entities with some form of relief from civil monetary penalties. Specifically, subsection 223(a) of the act required federal agencies regulating the activities of small entities to establish a policy or program by end of March 1997 for the reduction and, under appropriate circumstances, the waiver of civil penalties by small entities. In February 2001, GAO reported on the implementation of Section 223 and concluded that all of the agencies' penalty reduction and waiver policies were within the broad discretion afforded by the statute.[53] However, GAO also reported that some of the policies covered only a portion of the agencies' enforcement actions involving small entities, and some treated small entities no differently than large entities. The agencies' policies also differed in terms of how key terms such as "small entity" and "penalty reduction" were defined, and most were developed before SBREFA took effect. GAO suggested several changes to the statute to strengthen agencies' penalty relief policies and make them more consistent. For example, GAO suggested amending the act to require agencies to maintain data on the number of enforcement actions involving small entities and the amount of penalty relief provided. This recommendation was later implemented with the passage of the Small Business Paperwork Relief Act of 2002 (P.L. 107-198, 116 Stat. 729), which required (among other things) that agencies develop and report such information to selected congressional committees.

Congressional Review Act

The statutory provision commonly known as the Congressional Review Act (CRA) (5 U.S.C. §§801-808) was included as part of SBREFA as enacted in March 1996, and it established expedited procedures by which Congress may disapprove agencies' rules by enacting a joint resolution of disapproval.[54] Under the CRA, before any final rule can become effective it must be filed with each house of Congress and GAO.[55] The act also requires federal agencies to submit to GAO and make available to each house of Congress a copy of any cost-benefit analysis prepared for the rule and a report on the agency's actions related to the RFA and any other relevant act or executive order. The definition of a "rule" under the CRA is very broad, and the act applies to rules issued by Cabinet departments and independent agencies as well as independent regulatory agencies.

If OIRA considers the issuing agency's rule to be "major," the agency generally must delay the rule's effective date by 60 days after the date of publication in the *Federal Register* or submission to Congress and GAO, whichever is later.[56] Within 15 calendar days of receiving a major rule, GAO is required to provide Congress with a report on the rule assessing the issuing agency's compliance with the procedural steps required by the various acts and executive orders applicable to the rulemaking process.[57] Although the CRA establishes these special requirements for major rules, the CRA procedures for disapproving regulations apply to all rules, whether or not they are declared to be major.

Within 60 days after Congress receives an agency's rule, excluding periods when Congress is in recess or adjournment, a Member of Congress can introduce a resolution of disapproval that, if adopted by both Houses and enacted into law, can nullify the rule, even if it has already gone into effect. Congressional disapproval under the CRA also prevents the agency from proposing to issue a "substantially similar" rule without subsequent statutory authorization, but this provision is not intended to vitiate altogether the agency's power to establish regulations in the area in question.

The CRA provides that Senate action on a disapproval resolution under the act must occur within 60 days of session after the regulation is submitted, and it makes available during that period an expedited procedure intended to ensure that the Senate can take up and vote on the measure before the period expires. The act establishes no such expedited procedure for the House. If Congress adjourns less than 60 days of session after a rule is submitted, a new 60 day period for disapproval under the act begins on the 15th legislative day of the next session. If a disapproval resolution is rejected by either house of Congress, the rule can take effect immediately (or as provided by other governing law or rule).

Federal agencies have submitted more than 57,000 rules to GAO (and presumably, Congress) since the CRA took effect in March 1996, including more than 1,000 major rules. However, only one rule has been overturned through CRA's procedures—OSHA's ergonomics standard in March 2001 (P.L. 107-5). Many reasons have been suggested for why the CRA has not been used more often, but chief among them may be the fact that, if the President vetoes a resolution of disapproval (which is likely if the underlying rule is developed during his administration), then enactment of the resolution would require approval of a two-thirds majority in both houses of Congress to override the veto. The rejection of the ergonomics rule was the result of a specific set of circumstances created by a transition in party control of the presidency. The majority party in both houses of Congress was the same as the party of the incoming President (George W. Bush). The new Congress convened in 2001 and adopted a resolution disapproving the rule published under the outgoing President (William J. Clinton), which George W. Bush signed into law. Congress may be most able to use the CRA to disapprove rules in similar, transition-related circumstances.[58]

Congress can also stop agency rulemaking or regulatory enforcement through provisions added to agency appropriations legislation. There appear to be four types of such appropriations provisions: (1) restrictions on the finalization of particular proposed rules, (2) restrictions on regulatory activity within certain areas, (3) implementation or enforcement restrictions, and (4) conditional restrictions (e.g., preventing implementation of a rule until certain actions are taken). Some of these kinds of provisions have been included in appropriations bills for many years in a row. The reasons behind these restrictions vary, with some appearing to be based on economic considerations, some requiring or preventing the implementation of rules issued at the end of a presidential administration, and some included for various other reasons. Such provisions are generally applicable only for the period of time and the agencies covered by the relevant appropriations bill, but (depending on how they are worded) can be more broadly applicable. Also, to the extent that agencies have independent sources of funding (e.g., user fees) or implement their regulations through state or local governments, some of the limitations may not be as restrictive as they seem.[59]

Unfunded Mandates Reform Act

The Unfunded Mandates Reform Act (UMRA) of 1995 was enacted in an effort to reduce the costs associated with federal imposition of responsibilities, duties, and regulations upon state, local, and tribal governments and the private sector without providing the funding appropriate to the costs imposed by those responsibilities. Title I of UMRA established new procedures designed to ensure that Congress fully considers the potential effects of unfunded federal mandates before imposing them in legislation. Among other things, the procedures call for the Congressional Budget Office to provide statements to authorizing committees about whether reported bills contain mandates and, if so, the cost of those mandates.[60]

Title II of UMRA (2 U.S.C. §§1532-1538) contains requirements imposed on covered federal agencies during the rulemaking process. Specifically, the act requires Cabinet departments and independent agencies (but not independent regulatory agencies) to, among other things:

- prepare a written statement containing specific descriptions and estimates for any proposed rule or any final rule for which a proposed rule was published that includes any federal mandate that may result in the expenditure of $100 million or more in any year by state, local, or tribal governments, in the aggregate, or the private sector. One of the items required in the written statement is a qualitative and quantitative assessment of the anticipated costs and benefits of the mandate (Section 202);
- identify and consider a reasonable number of regulatory alternatives and select the least costly, most cost-effective, or least burdensome alternative (or explain why that alternative was not selected) for each rule for which a written statement is prepared (Section 205);
- develop a plan in which agencies provide notice of regulatory requirements to potentially affected small governments (Section 203); and
- develop an effective process to permit elected officers of state, local, and tribal governments (or their designees) to provide input in the development of regulatory proposals containing significant intergovernmental mandates (Section 204).

OIRA has primary responsibility for monitoring agency compliance with title II of UMRA, and issued guidance in March 1995 on the implementation of the title that generally repeated the requirements of the statute. OIRA also publishes an annual report on the implementation of title II.[61]

In February 1998, GAO reported that, because of the way the statute was written, title II of UMRA had little effect on agencies' rulemaking actions during its first two years of implementation.[62] First, many of the act's requirements did not appear to apply to most of the "economically significant" rules (e.g., rules with a $100 million impact on the economy) that were promulgated during this period. For example, if a final rule did not have an associated NPRM or imposed a mandate as a condition of federal financial assistance, the written statement requirement in Section 202 of UMRA does not apply. Second, UMRA does not require agencies to take the actions specified if the agencies determine that they are duplicative of other actions or that accurate estimates of the effect of their rules are not feasible. Third, even when UMRA is triggered, it often requires agencies to take actions that are identical or similar to actions that they were already required to take. For example, UMRA's requirements in sections 202 and 205 for the conduct of cost-benefit analysis and identification of regulatory alternatives are similar to the requirements that were already in place under Executive Order 12866, which was issued more than a year before UMRA was enacted. (See below for a discussion of "Executive Order 12866.") The consultation requirements in Section 204 are traceable to the notice and comment requirements in the APA, and are almost identical to the requirements in Executive Order 12875, which was issued more than a year before UMRA.

In May 2004, GAO again reported that UMRA's written statement requirements did not apply to most major or economically significant final rules issued in 2001 and 2002 (only 9 of 122).[63] However, GAO also said that some of the rules not triggering UMRA's requirements "appeared to have potential financial impacts on affected nonfederal parties similar to those of the actions that were identified as containing mandates at or above the act's thresholds." In March 2005, GAO reported that parties from various sectors (businesses, public interest groups, academia, and others) most commonly cited UMRA's numerous definitions, exclusions, and exceptions as problematic and in need of improvement.[64] In February 2011, GAO reiterated these conclusions, noting that there are 14 reasons why a rule may not be considered a "mandate" under UMRA.[65]

Information Quality Act

Section 515 of the Treasury and General Government Appropriations Act for Fiscal Year 2001 (P.L. 106-554), generally known as the "Data Quality Act" or the "Information Quality Act" (IQA), amended the Paperwork Reduction Act and directed OMB to issue government-wide guidelines that "provide policy and procedural guidance to Federal agencies for ensuring and maximizing the quality, objectivity, utility, and integrity of information (including statistical information) disseminated by Federal agencies."[66] The IQA also instructed agencies (both Cabinet departments and independent agencies as well as independent regulatory agencies) to issue their own guidelines not more than one year after the issuance of OMB's government-wide guidelines, and to establish administrative mechanisms allowing affected persons to seek and obtain correction of information maintained and disseminated by the agency. Finally, the act required agencies to report periodically to the Director of OMB on the number and nature of complaints received and how such complaints were handled by the agency. The first agency reports were due by January 1, 2004.

In response to a separate congressional requirement, in April 2004, OMB provided Congress with a report on the implementation of the IQA during FY2003.[67] The report said that agencies received only about 35 substantive correction requests during the year, and said it was "premature to make broad statements about both the impact of the correction request process and the overall responsiveness of the agencies." Many other correction requests listed in the report were on minor issues or involved matters that had been dealt with before the IQA was enacted. OMB indicated that the correction requests came from all segments of society, and said there was no evidence that the IQA had affected the pace of rulemaking. However, OMB Watch (a public interest group now known as the Center for Effective Government) said OMB's report was "seriously flawed" in that it understated the number of correction requests and did not disclose that nearly three-quarters of the requests were from industry.[68]

A major test of the IQA concerned whether agencies' denials of information correction requests are subject to judicial review. In March 2006, the U.S. Court of Appeals for the Fourth Circuit ruled that the act does not permit judicial review.[69] Two district courts had previously reached a similar conclusion, and the Department of Justice had issued a brief stating that the IQA does not permit judicial review.[70]

Peer Review

In a development closely related to the issue of information quality, in September 2003, OMB published a proposed bulletin on "Peer Review and Information Quality" that would have, if made final, provided a standardized process by which all significant regulatory information would be peer reviewed.[71] The authorities that OMB cited for this action were the IQA, the Paperwork Reduction Act, and Executive Order 12866. "Regulatory information" was defined in the bulletin as any scientific or technical study that "might" be used by federal, state, local, or international regulatory bodies.

Specifically, the bulletin proposed requiring each federal agency (each executive agency and independent regulatory agency) to take three actions: (1) have all "significant regulatory information" that it intends to disseminate peer reviewed (with information defined as "significant" if OMB determines that it will have a clear and substantial impact on important public policies or private sector decisions); (2) have "especially significant regulatory information" subject to the above requirements peer reviewed according to even higher standards (with information deemed "especially significant" if, among other things, it supports a regulatory action with a $100 million or more impact on the economy or "is relevant to an Administration policy priority"); and (3) provide OMB at least once each year with information about upcoming significant regulatory disseminations and the agency's plans for conducting peer reviews. The proposed bulletin also said agencies that are likely to disseminate "significant" or "especially significant" regulatory information must supplement or amend their information quality guidelines to incorporate the requirements of the proposed peer review bulletin for "significant" and "especially significant" information. The proposed bulletin indicated that OMB could waive the requirements for peer review if an agency made "a compelling case" that a waiver is necessary (e.g., an imminent health hazard or homeland security threat). OMB received 187 comments from the public and other agencies on its proposed peer review bulletin, with some supporting its issuance in final and others calling for its withdrawal and reconsideration. On April 15, 2004, OMB published a revised bulletin, and again asked the public for comments.[72]

On December 16, 2004, OMB published a final version of the peer review bulletin on its website.[73] The final bulletin was published in the *Federal Register* on January 14, 2005.[74] OMB said this version reflects "minor revisions" made in response to more than 50 comments from the public on the revised bulletin. For example, the final bulletin requires agencies to disclose the names of peer reviewers to the public and adds an annual reporting requirement to allow OMB to track how agencies are using the bulletin. However, agencies are still afforded substantial discretion to determine when and what type of peer review is required. OMB also retains substantial discretion in certain areas. As of June 2013, OMB has not updated or changed the peer review memo since it was finalized in December 2004.

OMB and supporters of the peer review bulletin indicate that peer review standards across the government are currently inconsistent, and that more consistent use of peer review can increase the technical quality and credibility of regulatory science.[75] They also assert that peer review can protect science-based regulations from political criticism and litigation. Opponents view the bulletin as an effort to inject political considerations into the world of science and to use the uncertainty that inevitably surrounds science as an excuse to delay new rules that could cost regulated entities millions or even billions of dollars. They also expressed concerns regarding the need for the bulletin and OMB's authority to issue it.[76]

Other Statutory Provisions Related to Rulemaking

Other statutory provisions have been enacted over the years that, while generally not imposing new rulemaking requirements per se, can affect the rulemaking process.

Federal Advisory Committee Act

Several statutes either require or permit the use of advisory committees in the federal rulemaking process. An advisory committee may be composed of experts in the regulatory field involved, representatives of the interest groups affected by the rule, and related federal or state agencies, and may help set the agency's rulemaking agenda or may simply serve as a sounding board for agency ideas. The enactment of the Federal Advisory Committee Act (FACA) of 1972 (5 U.S.C. App. II) established requirements to ensure that agencies using advisory committees receive impartial and relevant expertise. Specifically, FACA requires that the advice provided by advisory committees be objective and accessible to the public. With certain exceptions, each advisory committee meeting is presumptively open to the public. Adequate advance notice of the meetings must be published in the *Federal Register*, and all papers, records, and minutes of the meetings must generally be made available to the public. FACA also requires that the advisory committees be fairly balanced in regard to the points of view of affected interests and the functions performed. The act defines an advisory committee as any committee or similar group (1) established or used to obtain advice or recommendation for one or more federal agencies or the President and (2) that is not composed wholly of full-time federal officers or employees.[77]

Trade Agreements Act

The Trade Agreements Act of 1979 (19 U.S.C. §§2531-2533) prohibits agencies from setting regulatory standards that create "unnecessary obstacles to foreign commerce" of the United States. The act specifically states that legitimate domestic objectives such as safety or health are not considered unnecessary obstacles. The statute also requires, where appropriate, the use of performance standards rather than design standards and the consideration of international standards as the basis of domestic standards.

Negotiated Rulemaking Act

The Negotiated Rulemaking Act of 1990 (5 U.S.C. §§561-570a), as amended and permanently authorized in 1996 (110 Stat. 3870), seeks to overcome what some observers describe as an adversarial relationship between agencies and affected interest groups that often accompanies agency rulemaking. The concept of negotiated rulemaking (sometimes referred to as regulatory negotiation or "reg-neg") emerged in the 1980s as a supplement to the traditional procedure for developing regulations. Negotiated rulemaking does not replace procedures necessary under the APA. Instead, the act encourages (but does not require) agencies to consider convening a negotiated rulemaking committee before developing and issuing a proposed regulation under the APA. The committee, composed of representatives of the agency and the various interest groups that would be affected by the proposed regulation, addresses areas of concern in the hope that it can reach agreement on the contents of a proposed regulation. The agency can, if it agrees, then issue the agreement as a proposed rule, and eventually a final rule under existing APA requirements. The expectation is that any rule drafted through negotiated rulemaking would be easier to implement and less likely to be the subject of subsequent litigation. However, any proposal agreed to by the negotiated rulemaking committee is not binding on the agency or other parties.

The major provisions of the act require that (1) a negotiated rulemaking committee consist of at least one member of the agency and no more than 25 members, unless the head of the agency determines that more are needed; (2) the agency select an impartial "facilitator" to chair meetings, subject to the approval of the committee by consensus; (3) an agreement on any negotiated rulemaking must be unanimous, unless the negotiated rulemaking committee agrees to other conditions; and (4) the head of an agency, when deciding whether to establish a negotiated rulemaking committee, assure that (a) there are a limited number of identifiable interests that will be significantly affected by the rule; (b) there is a reasonable chance that a committee can be convened with a balanced representation of interested parties willing to negotiate in good faith; and (c) there is a reasonable likelihood that a committee will reach a consensus on the proposed rule within a fixed period of time.

An agency may pay reasonable travel and *per diem* expenses, and reasonable compensation to negotiating committee members under certain conditions. The agency must comply with FACA in establishing and administering the committee. Agency procedural actions related to establishing, assisting, or terminating the committee are not subject to judicial review, but any judicial review available regarding the rule resulting from negotiated rulemaking is unaffected.[78] Although the use of negotiated rulemaking was expected to improve rulemaking timeliness and reduce litigation, one examination of agencies' efforts in this area indicated that those expectations were not being fulfilled.[79] However, another study indicated that negotiated rulemaking can improve participants' perception of the final rule and of the overall rulemaking process.[80]

Although the Negotiated Rulemaking Act gives agencies substantial discretion as to whether the approach should be employed in rulemaking, Congress has sometimes mandated its use by rulemaking agencies and established specific procedures and time frames to follow. For example, Section 5602 of the Patient Protection and Affordable Care Act requires the Secretary of Health and Human Services to use negotiated rulemaking to establish a "comprehensive methodology and criteria for designation of ... (A) medically underserved populations in accordance with section 330(b)(3) of the Public Health Service Act (42 U.S.C. § 254b(b)(3))," and "(B) health professions shortage areas under section 332 of the Public Health Service Act (42 U.S.C. § 254e)."[81]

National Technology Transfer and Advancement Act

Section 12(d) of the National Technology Transfer and Advancement Act (15 U.S.C. §272 note), adopted in March 1996, generally requires federal agencies to "use technical standards that are developed or adopted by voluntary consensus standards bodies" to carry out policy objectives unless doing so is "inconsistent with applicable law or otherwise impractical." Agencies are also required to consult with and (if in the public interest and compatible with agency missions, authority, priorities, and resources) participate with voluntary, private sector, consensus bodies. This provision essentially codified policies already in existence in OMB Circular A-119, and also established reporting requirements and authorized the National Institute of Standards and Technology (NIST) within the Department of Commerce to coordinate agencies' conformity assessment activities. According to NIST, federal agencies use consensus standards in hundreds of federal procurement or regulatory programs (e.g., requiring certification from Underwriters Laboratories that a product is safe or requiring individuals in certain professions meet specific educational or competency standards).[82]

Regulatory Right-to-Know Act

Section 624 of the Treasury and General Government Appropriations Act, 2001 (31 U.S.C. §1105 note), sometimes referred to as the "Regulatory Right-to-Know Act," requires OMB to prepare and submit with the budget an "accounting statement and associated report" containing an estimate of the total costs and benefits (including quantifiable and nonquantifiable effects) of federal rules and paperwork, to the extent feasible, (1) in the aggregate, (2) by agency and agency program, and (3) by major rule. The accounting statement is also to contain an analysis of impacts of federal regulation on state, local, and tribal governments, small businesses, wages, and economic growth. The statute requires an accounting statement and report for calendar year 2002 "and each year thereafter."[83] To prepare the report, OMB relies heavily on agencies' estimates of costs and benefits for individual rules published during the previous 10 years. However, if an agency quantified but did not monetize its estimates, OMB monetizes them using "standard" assumptions. In its reports, OMB attempts to capture the agencies' nonquantified benefits and costs in "other information" columns, but OMB's monetized estimates exclude these effects.[84]

Government Paperwork Elimination Act

In 1998, Congress enacted the Government Paperwork Elimination Act (GPEA) (44 U.S.C. §3504 note), which required that by October 21, 2003, federal agencies provide the public, when practicable, with the option of submitting, maintaining, and disclosing information electronically, instead of on paper. GPEA makes OMB responsible for ensuring that federal agencies meet the act's implementation deadline. Although GPEA does not specifically mention rulemaking, both OMB and rulemaking agencies have indicated that its requirements have provided an impetus for developing information technology-based approaches to rulemaking that involves information collection and, more generally, to regulatory management.

E-Government Act

The E-Government Act of 2002 (44 U.S.C.A. §3601 note) was designed to enhance the management and promotion of electronic government services and processes, and contains requirements affecting the rulemaking process. Specifically, Section 206 of the act requires agencies, to the extent practicable, to:

- ensure that a publicly accessible website includes all information about that agency that is required to be published in the *Federal Register*,
- accept public comments on proposed rules "by electronic means," and
- ensure that a publicly accessible federal website contains "electronic dockets" for proposed rules containing all comments submitted on the rules as well as "other materials that by agency rule or practice are included in the rulemaking docket under (the APA), whether or not submitted electronically."

The E-Government Act also requires agencies to conduct a "privacy impact assessment" before initiating a new collection of information that uses information technology and contains individually identifying information. In addition, the act established an Office of Electronic Government within OMB, headed by an Administrator appointed by the President. It requires the Administrator of that office to work with the Administrator of OIRA in establishing the strategic direction of the e-government program, and to oversee its implementation.

In January 2003, the Bush Administration launched the "Regulations.gov" website, an "erulemaking" initiative intended to accomplish many of the objectives of the E-Government Act. Regulations.gov has electronic versions of proposed and final rules, as well as other rulemaking documents and *Federal Register* notices, and the public can identify and submit comments electronically on rules that are open for comment.[85] The Environmental Protection Agency (EPA) is the managing agency for *Regulations.gov.*[86]

Small Business Paperwork Relief Act

In June 2002, Congress enacted and the President signed the Small Business Paperwork Relief Act of 2002 (P.L. 107-198). The act amended the Paperwork Reduction Act to, among other things, require each agency to establish a single point of contact to act as a liaison for small business concerns with regard to information collection and paperwork issues. It also directed agencies to make a special effort to reduce information collection burdens for small businesses with fewer than 25 employees. OMB was directed to publish in the *Federal Register* and make available on the Internet an annual list of the compliance assistance resources available to small businesses.[87] The act also required agencies to report to Congress on the amount of penalty relief provided to small businesses, and established a task force to study the feasibility of streamlining information collection requirements on small businesses.

EXECUTIVE ORDERS AND DIRECTIVES

During the past 20 years, each President has issued executive orders and/or presidential directives designed to guide the federal rulemaking process, often with the goal of reducing regulatory burden. Although independent regulatory agencies are generally not covered by these requirements, they are often encouraged to follow them. By far the most important of the current executive rulemaking requirements is Executive Order 12866,[88] which describes both the principles and the process by which presidential regulatory review currently takes place.

Executive Order 12866

Centralized review of agencies' regulations within the Executive Office of the President has been part of the federal rulemaking process for more than 30 years. Although each of his three predecessors had some type of review process, the most significant development in the evolution of presidential review of rulemaking occurred in 1981, when President Reagan issued Executive Order 12291. The executive order established a set of general requirements for rulemaking, and required federal agencies (other than independent regulatory agencies) to send a copy of each draft proposed and final rule to OMB before publication in the *Federal Register*. It also required covered agencies to prepare a regulatory impact analysis for each "major" rule (e.g., those with a $100 million impact on the economy). As a result of this order, OIRA's responsibilities were greatly expanded from paperwork reviews under the Paperwork Reduction Act to examinations of the substance of covered agencies rules—between 2,000 and 3,000 reviews per year. In 1985, President Reagan expanded OIRA's influence further by issuing Executive Order 12498, which required covered agencies (all except independent regulatory agencies) to submit a regulatory plan to OMB for review each year that covered all of their significant regulatory actions underway or planned.

On September 30, 1993, President Clinton issued Executive Order 12866, which revoked Executive Orders 12291 and 12498 and established a new process for OIRA review of rules.[89] Like its predecessors, the new executive order limited OIRA's reviews to proposed and final rules published by agencies other than independent regulatory agencies. However, it also limited OIRA reviews to actions identified by the rulemaking agency or OIRA as "significant" regulatory actions, defined as those that were "economically significant" (e.g., those with a $100 million impact on the economy) or that (1) were inconsistent or interfered with an action taken or planned by another agency; (2) materially altered the budgetary impact of entitlements, grants, user fees, or loan programs; or (3) raised novel legal or policy issues. As a result, the number of rules that OIRA reviewed dropped from between 2,000 and 3,000 per year to between 500 and 700 per year.

Executive Order 12866 also differs from its predecessors in other respects. For example, the order requires that OIRA generally complete its reviews of proposed and final rules within 90 calendar days. It also requires both rulemaking agencies and OIRA to disclose certain information about how the regulatory reviews were conducted. For example, agencies are to identify for the public (1) the substantive changes made to rules between the draft submitted to OIRA for review and the action subsequently announced, and (2) changes made at the suggestion or recommendation of OIRA. OIRA is required to, among other things, provide agencies with a copy of all communications between OIRA personnel and parties outside of the executive branch, and to maintain a public log of all regulatory actions under review and of all of the documents provided to the agencies.[90]

For each significant draft rule, the executive order requires the issuing agency to provide to OIRA the text of the draft rule, a description of why the rule is needed, and a general assessment of the rule's costs and benefits. For draft rules that are "economically significant," the executive order requires a detailed cost-benefit analysis, including an assessment of the costs and benefits of "potentially effective and reasonably feasible alternatives to the planned regulation." One of the "principles of regulation" in the order is that agencies shall "propose or adopt a regulation only upon a reasoned determination that the benefits of the intended regulation justify its costs." The order also says that when setting regulatory priorities, "each agency shall consider, to the extent reasonable, the degree and nature of the risks posed by various substances or activities within its jurisdiction." The executive order's "regulatory philosophy" states that unless a statute requires another regulatory approach, "in choosing among alternative regulatory approaches, agencies should select those approaches that maximize net benefits."[91]

During the formal Executive Order 12866 review process, OIRA analyzes the draft rule in light of the principles of the executive order and discusses the rule with staff and officials at the rulemaking agency. OIRA may also discuss the draft rule with other agencies with whom interagency coordination will be necessary, and may meet or otherwise communicate with interested stakeholders outside of the federal government.[92] At the end of the review, OIRA either concludes that the draft rule is consistent with the principles of the executive order (the majority of the cases) or returns the rule to the agency "for further consideration." In some cases agencies withdraw their draft rules during OIRA's review. If the draft is a proposed rule, the agency may then publish an NPRM. If the draft is a final rule, the agency may then publish a final rule and allow the rule to take effect. OIRA staff also sometimes review draft rules informally before their formal submission under the executive order—particularly when there is a statutory or legal deadline or when a rule has a large impact on society.

OIRA's formal review process has not changed substantially since Executive Order 12866 was issued in 1993.[93] However, GAO reported in September 2003 that there were several changes in OIRA policies and practices when then-OIRA Administrator John Graham took office in July 2001, including (1) increased use of public letters explaining why OIRA returned rules to agencies for their consideration and suggesting regulatory action, (2) increased emphasis on cost-benefit analysis and peer review of agencies' rules, (3) stricter adherence to the 90-day time limit for OIRA review, (4) improvements in the transparency of the OIRA review process, and (5) an increase in the size and skills of OIRA's staff.[94] Underlying many of these changes is a shift in how OIRA administrators view the office's role in the rulemaking process—from "counselor" to the agencies to regulatory "gatekeeper." GAO also concluded that, certain changes notwithstanding, the

OIRA review process was still not very transparent to the public, and recommended several changes in OIRA's disclosure policies. In a 2009 report, GAO again recommended changes and improvements in the transparency of OIRA reviews under Executive Order 12866.[95]

Executive Order 12866 also includes several other notable requirements. For example, Section 5 of the order requires agencies to periodically review their existing significant regulations to determine whether they should be modified or eliminated. In March 1995, President Clinton reemphasized this requirement by directing each agency to conduct a page-by-page review of all existing regulations. In June 1995, the President announced that 16,000 pages had been eliminated from the *Code of Federal Regulations*. GAO reported on this review effort in October 1997, noting that the page elimination totals that four agencies reported did not take into account pages that had been added while the eliminations took place.[96] GAO also reported that about half of the actions taken appeared to have no effect on the burden felt by regulated entities, would have little effect, or could increase regulatory burden.

Executive Order 13422

On January 18, 2007, President George W. Bush issued Executive Order 13422, making the most significant amendments to Executive Order 12866 since it was published. The major changes made by Executive Order 13422 fell into five general categories: (1) a requirement that agencies identify in writing the specific market failure or problem that warrants a new regulation, (2) a requirement that each agency head designate a presidential appointee within the agency as a "regulatory policy officer" who can control upcoming rulemaking activity in that agency, (3) a requirement that agencies provide their best estimates of the cumulative regulatory costs and benefits of rules they expect to publish in the coming year, (4) an expansion of OIRA review to include significant guidance documents,[97] and (5) a provision permitting agencies to consider whether to use more formal rulemaking procedures in certain cases.

On January 30, 2009, President Barack Obama issued Executive Order 13497, which (among other things) revoked Executive Order 13422.[98] As a result, Executive Order 12866 was returned to its original form as issued in September 1993.

Executive Order 13563

On January 18, 2011, President Obama issued Executive Order 13563 on "Improving Regulation and Regulatory Review."[99] Section 1(b) of the new order states that "This order is supplemental to and reaffirms the principles, structures, and definitions governing contemporary regulatory review that were established in Executive Order 12866 of September 30, 1993." Although similar to the 1993 order in many respects, Executive Order 13563 contains some new provisions. For example, Section 2(b) of the order states that agencies should generally provide "timely online access to the rulemaking docket on *regulations.gov,* including relevant scientific and technical findings, in an open format that can be easily searched and downloaded. For proposed rules, such access shall include, to the extent feasible and permitted by law, an opportunity for public comment on all pertinent parts of the rulemaking docket, including relevant scientific and technical findings."

Perhaps most notably, Section 6(b) of the new order requires agencies to initiate retrospective reviews of their existing rules. Specifically, it states,

> Within 120 days of the date of this order, each agency shall develop and submit to the Office of Information and Regulatory Affairs a preliminary plan, consistent with law and its resources and regulatory priorities, under which the agency will periodically review its existing significant regulations to determine whether any such regulations should be modified, streamlined, expanded, or repealed so as to make the agency's regulatory program more effective or less burdensome in achieving the regulatory objectives.

Section 5(a) of Executive Order 12866 had previously required agencies to submit a plan for retrospective reviews to OIRA, so this provision appears to require agencies to update those plans.[100] On February 2, 2011, the OIRA Administrator issued guidance to federal agencies on the implementation of the executive order, including these retrospective reviews.[101]

Executive Order 13579

As a follow-up to Executive Order 13563, President Obama issued Executive Order 13579, asking independent regulatory agencies to follow the key principles of Executive Order 13563 and to produce plans for retrospective analysis of their existing rules.[102]

Other Executive Orders and Directives

Agencies other than independent regulatory agencies must also be aware of an array of other rulemaking requirements contained in executive orders and presidential directives. For example:

- Executive Order 13132 on "Federalism" requires covered federal agencies to "have an accountable process to ensure meaningful and timely input by State and local officials in the development of regulatory policies that have federalism implications."[103] The order defines "federalism implications" as "substantial direct effects on the States, on the relationship between the national government and the States, or on the distribution of power and responsibilities among the various levels of government." Federal agencies are prohibited from promulgating any regulation with unfunded federalism implications unless they have (1) consulted with state and local officials early in the development of the proposed rule, and (2) prepared a "federalism summary impact statement" consisting of a description of the prior consultation with state and local officials, a summary of their concerns and the agency's position regarding the need to issue the rule, and a statement of the extent to which the officials' concerns have been met. The order gives agencies substantial discretion regarding its implementation. For example, it does not define what type of regulatory action constitutes "substantial direct effects," and says the consultation and impact statement requirements apply "to the extent practicable."[104]
- Executive Order 12630 on constitutionally protected property rights says each agency "shall be guided by" certain principles when formulating or implementing policies that have "takings" implications.[105] For example, the order says that private property should be taken only for "real and substantial threats," and "be no greater than is necessary."[106]
- Executive Order 12889 on the North American Free Trade Agreement generally requires agencies subject to the APA to provide at least a 75-day comment period for any "proposed Federal technical regulation or any Federal sanitary or phytosanitary measure of general application."[107]
- Executive Order 12898 on environmental justice says (among other things) that each agency must develop a strategy that identifies and

addresses disproportionately high and adverse human health or environmental effects of its programs, policies, and activities on minority populations and low income populations.[108] It also says that environmental human health research should include diverse segments of the population in epidemiological and clinical studies, and that agencies should identify rules that should be revised to meet the objectives of the order.

- Executive Order 12988 on civil justice reform generally requires agencies reviewing existing and new regulations to ensure that they comply with specific requirements (e.g., "eliminate drafting errors and ambiguity" and "provide a clear legal standard for affected conduct") to improve regulatory drafting in order to minimize litigation.[109] Agencies formulating proposed regulations are directed to "make every reasonable effort" to ensure that they, among other things, specify in clear language any preemptive or retroactive effects, and the effect on existing law.
- Executive Order 13045 on protection of children from environmental health risks and safety risks says that for any substantive rulemaking action that is likely to result in an economically significant rule that concerns an environmental health risk or safety risk that may disproportionately affect children, the agency must provide OIRA with (1) an evaluation of the environmental or safety effects on children and (2) an explanation of why the planned regulation is preferable to other potentially effective and reasonably feasible alternatives.[110]
- Executive Order 13175 on consultation and coordination with Indian tribal governments generally prohibits agencies from promulgating any regulation not required by law that has tribal implications and imposes substantial direct costs on tribal governments unless the necessary funds are provided or the agency consults with tribal officials and provides a "tribal summary impact statement" describing those consultations.[111] Similar consultation and impact statement requirements apply to rules that preempt tribal laws.
- Executive Order 13211 on energy impacts requires agencies (to the extent permitted by law) to prepare and submit to OMB a "statement of energy effects" for significant energy actions.[112] The statement, published in the NPRM and the final rule, is to include a detailed statement of "any adverse effects on energy supply, distribution, or use" for the action and reasonable alternatives and their effects.

- Executive Order 13272 on small entities generally requires federal agencies to issue (by February 2003) written procedures and policies to ensure proper consideration during the rulemaking process of the impacts of their draft rules on small entities.[113] The order also requires agencies to notify the SBA Chief Counsel for Advocacy of any draft rules that may have a significant economic impact on a substantial number of small entities, and to give "every appropriate consideration" to any comments the Chief Counsel provides.
- Executive Order 13609 requires agencies, as well as a "Regulatory Working Group," to consider the issue of international regulatory cooperation and how to eliminate differences in regulations between the United States and its major trading partners.[114]
- Executive Order 13610 instructs agencies to institutionalize regular reviews of their previously issued significant regulations, and to take additional steps to increase public participation in retrospective reviews of regulations.[115]

In addition to executive orders, presidential memoranda or directives can also affect the rulemaking process. For example:

- a March 4, 1995, presidential memorandum directed federal agencies to (among other things) focus their regulatory programs on results, not process, and expand their use of negotiated rulemaking.
- an April 21, 1995, memorandum directed agencies to waive or reduce penalties in certain circumstances, and to reduce the frequency of reports the public is required to provide to the government.
- a June 1, 1998, presidential directive required agencies to use plain language in proposed and final rulemaking documents.

CONCLUSION

During the past 60 to 65 years, Congress and various Presidents have made numerous attempts to add structure, economy, efficiency, accountability, and greater public access and transparency to the regulatory process. In this regard, Congress has enacted laws such as the Administrative Procedure Act, the Regulatory Flexibility Act, the Paperwork Reduction Act, and the Unfunded Mandates Reform Act that require some type of procedure, review, and/or analysis of draft rules by the rulemaking agencies themselves or by outside parties. Presidential rulemaking requirements have often focused on coordination of agencies' regulatory efforts with the President's priorities and attempts to improve the quality of regulations through cost-benefit analysis, risk assessment analysis, and the consideration of specific factors in the rulemaking process (e.g., environmental justice, children, and property rights). Underlying many of these congressional and presidential requirements is an attempt to ensure that certain interests or issues are considered during the rulemaking process and/or to minimize the burden associated with federal regulations. However, these rulemaking requirements impose burdens of their own on rulemaking agencies, and may be a factor in the length of time it takes agencies to issue rules. Federal agencies must be aware of the cross-cutting and the program-specific statutory and executive requirements underlying their regulations and must craft rules that are consistent with those requirements—or run the risk of having their rules returned to them by OIRA or rejected by Congress or the courts. Several of these statutes and orders indicate that their requirements may be integrated with or satisfied by the requirements in other statutes or orders. For example, the Regulatory Flexibility Act states that federal agencies can develop their regulatory agendas and perform their regulatory flexibility analyses "in conjunction with or as a part of any other agenda or analysis required by any other law." Some observers believe that integration and consolidation of all these requirements could improve the rulemaking process. In 1993 the Administrative Conference of the United States noted that the simple requirements in the Administrative Procedure Act for informal rulemaking had been "overlain with an increasing number of constraints," including those imposed by Congress, Presidents, and the courts. The Administrative Conference recommended a "coordinated framework of proposals aimed at promoting efficient and effective rulemaking."[116] Since then, the number of rulemaking requirements has increased.

On the other hand, many of these statutory and executive order provisions provide the agencies substantial discretion regarding when and how the rulemaking requirements are to be applied. For example, because the Regulatory Flexibility Act does not define the term "significant impact on a substantial number of small entities," agencies have a great deal of latitude to determine when a regulatory flexibility analysis is required. Similarly, Executive Order 13132 does not define the term "significant federalism implications," so agencies have substantial discretion in deciding whether the analytical requirements of the order have been triggered. Other rulemaking requirements are written in such a way that they actually apply to only a small number of rules. For example, title II of the Unfunded Mandates Reform Act does not apply to any rules published by independent regulatory agencies or any rules for which an agency determines there is "good cause" not to publish a notice of proposed rulemaking. Other rules are exempt from UMRA if they are conditions of federal financial assistance or enforce constitutional rights. Finally, if agencies are not required to prepare regulatory flexibility analyses for their proposed rules, they are also exempt from the SBREFA requirements to prepare small entity compliance guides and (in the case of OSHA, EPA, and CFPB) to convene advocacy review panels.

Because of the inevitability of regulation and its associated burden, efforts to either tighten existing requirements or impose new ones are likely to continue. A clear understanding of the existing requirements and how they have been implemented may inform any such future efforts.

FOR ADDITIONAL INFORMATION

Cornelius M. Kerwin and Scott R. Furlong, *Rulemaking: How Government Agencies Write Law and Make Policy, Fourth Edition* (Washington: CQ Press, 2011).

Jeffrey S. Lubbers, *A Guide To Federal Agency Rulemaking, Fifth Edition* (Chicago: ABA Publishing, 2012).

In addition, information regarding a variety of regulatory issues is available at the following websites:

Center for Progressive Regulation
http://www.progressiveregulation.org

Center for Regulatory Effectiveness
http://www.thecre.com

Competitive Enterprise Institute
http://www.cei.org

Government Accountability Office (GAO, formerly the General Accounting Office)
http://www.gao.gov

Government Printing Office (GPO)
http://www.gpo.gov/fdsys/search/home.action

Office of Management and Budget
http://www.whitehouse.gov/omb

Center for Effective Government (formerly OMB Watch)
http://www.foreffectivegov.org/

Regulations.gov
http://www.regulations.gov

Regulatory Information Service Center
http://www.reginfo.gov

End Notes

[1] Colin Diver, "Regulatory Precision," in Keith Hawkins and John Thomas, eds., Making Regulatory Policy (Pittsburgh: University of Pittsburgh Press, 1989), p. 199.

[2] Cornelius M. Kerwin, Rulemaking: How Government Agencies Write Law and Make Public Policy, 4th ed., (Washington: CQ Press, 2011), p. 2.

[3] 5 U.S.C. §551(4). The APA itself is 5 U.S.C. §§551 et seq.

[4] As used in this report, the term "independent regulatory agencies" refers to the boards and commissions identified as such in the Paperwork Reduction Act (44 U.S.C. §3502(5)), including the Federal Communications Commission, the Federal Energy Regulatory Commission, the Nuclear Regulatory Commission, and the Securities and Exchange Commission. The term "independent agencies" refers to other agencies that answer directly to the President, but are not part of Cabinet departments.

[5] See, for example, Thomas O. McGarity, "Some Thoughts on 'Deossifying' the Rulemaking Process, Duke Law Journal, vol. 41 (June 1992), pp. 1385-1462; Richard J. Pierce, Jr., "Seven Ways to Deossify Agency Rulemaking," 47 Administrative Law Review, vol. 47, winter 1995, pp. 59-93; Paul R. Verkuil, "Rulemaking Ossification—A Modest Proposal," Administrative Law Review, vol. 47 (summer 1995), pp. 453-459.

[6] National Advisory Committee on Occupational Safety and Health, Report and Recommendations Related to OSHA's Standards Development Process (Washington: June 6, 2000).

[7] For example, 29 U.S.C. §1306(a)(3)(A) states that the annual premium rate payable in the case of a single-employer plan for basic benefits is "an amount equal to the sum of $19 plus the additional premium (if any) determined under subparagraph (E) for each individual who is a participant in such plan during the plan year."

[8] DOT's 1998 appropriations act stated that "(n)one of the funds in this Act shall be available to prepare, propose, or promulgate any regulations ... in any model year that differs from the standards promulgated for such automobiles prior to the enactment of this section."

[9] For an examination of the amount of regulatory discretion afforded in specific statutes, see U.S. General Accounting Office, Regulatory Burden: Some Agencies' Claims Regarding Lack of Rulemaking Discretion Have Merit, GAO/GGD-99-20, January 8, 1999.

[10] For more information on PPACA rulemaking provisions, see CRS Report R41180, Rulemaking Requirements and Authorities in the Patient Protection and Affordable Care Act (PPACA), by Curtis W. Copeland. The author is no longer at CRS; questions about this report can be directed to Maeve P. Carey, Analyst in Government Organization and Management.

[11] Industrial Union Department v. American Petroleum Institute, 448 U.S. 607 (1980).

[12] See, for example, American Textile Mfrs. Inst., Inc. v. Donovan, 452 U.S. 490 (1981) and United Steelworkers v. Marshall, 647 F.2d 1189 (D.C. Cir. 1980), cert. denied, 453 U.S. 913 (1981).

[13] See, for example, Motor Vehicle Manufacturers Association v. State Farm Mutual Automobile Insurance Co., 463 U.S. 29 (1983). The Supreme Court said the agency "must examine the relevant data and articulate a satisfactory explanation of its action, including a 'rational connection between the facts found and the choice made.'"

[14] 1 C.F.R. ch. I, pts. 1-22.

[15] Electronic access to the Federal Register is provided through the Government Printing Office website at http://www.gpo.gov/fdsys/search/advanced/advsearchpage.action.

[16] United States v. Florida East Coast Railway, 410 U.S. 224 (1973).

[17] For more on formal and other types of rulemaking, as well as information on judicial review, see CRS Report R41546, A Brief Overview of Rulemaking and Judicial Review, by Todd Garvey and Daniel T. Shedd.

[18] Some agencies begin the rulemaking process by publishing an "advance notice of proposed rulemaking" in which the agency notifies the public that it is considering an area for rulemaking and often requests comments on the appropriate scope or topics of the rule. The APA does not require the use of advance notices, but some other statutes require it for particular types of rules. Similarly, agencies may issue a "supplemental notice of proposed rulemaking" after an NPRM is issued if they wish to obtain public comment on new factual proposals before issuing a final rule.

[19] Executive Order 12866, discussed in detail later in this report, suggests that agencies allow the public at least 60 days to comment for "significant" rules.

[20] The APA judicial review provisions are codified at 5 U.S.C 701-706. For more information on the APA and judicial review, see CRS Report R41546, A Brief Overview of Rulemaking and Judicial Review, by Todd Garvey and Daniel T. Shedd.

[21] In addition to the APA exceptions, Congress sometimes includes specific exemptions from notice and comment procedures in other statutes. For example, Section 161(d) under title I of the Federal Agriculture Improvement and Reform Act of 1996 (P.L. 104-127, 110 Stat. 934-935) instructed the Secretary of Agriculture and the Commodity Credit Corporation to issue regulations not later than 90 days after the date of enactment of the title, without regard to the notice and comment provisions of the APA.

[22] Senate Committee on the Judiciary, "Administrative Procedure Act: Legislative History," Senate Document 248, 79th Congress, 2nd Session (1946).

[23] For discussions of these court cases, see Ellen R. Jordan, "The Administrative Procedure Act's 'Good Cause' Exemption," Administrative Law Review, 36, spring 1984, pp. 113-178; and Catherine J. Lanctot, "The Good Cause Exception: Danger to Notice and Comment Requirements Under the Administrative Procedure Act," Georgetown Law Journal, 68 (February 1980), pp. 765-782.

[24] See American Federation of Government Employees, AFL-CIO v. Block, 655 F.2d 1153, 1156 (D.C. Cir 1981); and Mobay Chemical Corp. v. Gorsuch, (682 F.2d 419, 426 (3rd Cir.), cert. denied, 459 U.S. 988 (1982). In another case (Action on Smoking and Health v. CAB, 713 F.2d 795, 800 [D.C. Cir 1983]), the court said that allowing broad use of the good cause exception would "carve the heart out of the statute."

[25] For more, see Ronald M. Levin, "More on Direct Final Rulemaking: Streamlining, Not Corner Cutting," Administrative Law Review, 51 (summer 1999), pp. 757-766.

[26] See Office of the Vice President, Improving Regulatory Systems: Accompanying Report of the National Performance Review (Washington: September 1993). The Administrative Conference was established by statute as an independent agency to promote improvements in the efficiency, adequacy, and fairness of procedures by which federal agencies conduct regulatory programs, administer grants and benefits, and perform related governmental functions.

[27] For more, see Michael Asimow, "Interim Final Rules: Making Haste Slowly," Administrative Law Review, 51 (summer 1999), pp. 703-755.

[28] U.S. General Accounting Office, Federal Rulemaking: Agencies Often Published Final Actions Without Proposed Rules, GAO/GGD-98-126, August 31, 1998.

[29] See Juan J. Lavilla, "The Good Cause Exemption to Notice and Comment Rulemaking Requirements Under the Administrative Procedure Act," The Administrative Law Journal, 3 (fall 1989), pp. 317-423 for another study on the use of the good cause exception.

[30] NEPA regulations are codified at 40 CFR Parts 1500-1508.

[31] NEPA Task Force, Report to the Council on Environmental Quality, Modernizing NEPA Implementation (Washington: September 2003).

[32] For more information this legislation and on NEPA, see CRS Report RL33152, The National Environmental Policy Act (NEPA): Background and Implementation, by Linda Luther.

[33] For example, EPA's Toxics Release Inventory (TRI) program is essentially a database created through collections of information imposed on businesses to inform the public about chemical hazards in their communities. TRI reports require businesses in certain industries to report the quantity of any of more than 600 chemicals entering each environmental medium on site, transfers of the chemical in wastes to off-site locations, on-site treatment methods and efficiency, and source reduction and recycling activities.

[34] For an up-to-date inventory of OMB-approved information collections, see http://www.reginfo.gov/public/do/ PRAMain.

[35] Independent regulatory agencies can, by majority vote, void any OIRA disapproval of a proposed collection of information.

[36] An agency's annual paperwork burden-hour estimate is a function of (1) the frequency of the information collection, (2) the estimated number of respondents, and (3) amount of time that the agency estimates it takes each respondent to complete the collection. For example, if an agency estimates that an information collection conducted twice each year will take each of the estimated 10,000 respondents 10 hours to complete each time, the total annual burden hour estimate for the collection is 200,000 burden hours (2 times 10,000 times 10).

[37] The act's definition of an agency excludes only the General Accounting Office, the Federal Election Commission, the governments of the District of Columbia, U.S. territories and possessions, and government-owned contractor-operated facilities.

[38] OMB is required to report to Congress on the implementation of the PRA, and does so through an annual "information collection budget." For the 2012 report, see http://www.whitehouse.gov/sites/default/files/omb/inforeg/ icb/icb_2012.pdf.

[39] For more information on the PRA, see CRS Report R40636, Paperwork Reduction Act (PRA): OMB and Agency Responsibilities and Burden Estimates, by Curtis W. Copeland and Vanessa K. Burrows. The authors of this report are no longer at CRS. Questions about its content can be directed to Maeve P. Carey.

[40] See http://www.reginfo.gov/public/do/PRAMain for information collection totals.

[41] Many agencies are apparently aware of this limitation; GAO estimated that in more than 500 final rules published in 1997, the agencies specifically stated that the RFA was not applicable or that a regulatory flexibility analysis was not required because the action was not preceded by an NPRM. See GAO/GGD-98-126, p. 31.

[42] U.S. Small Business Administration, 20 Years of the Regulatory Flexibility Act: Rulemaking in a Dynamic Economy (Washington: 2000).

[43] This requirement, as well as a similar requirement in Executive Order 12866, is generally met via entries in the Unified Agenda of Federal Regulatory and Deregulatory Actions. The Unified Agenda is published twice each year in the Federal Register by the Regulatory Information Service Center, and provides uniform reporting of data on regulatory activities under development throughout the federal government.

[44] Amendments to the RFA enacted in 1996 added these requirements for EPA and OSHA, and the Dodd-Frank Wall Street Reform and Consumer Protection Act (P.L. 111-203) added the requirement for the CFPB.

[45] For an examination of the first five advocacy review panels were implemented, see U.S. General Accounting Office, Regulatory Reform: Implementation of the Small Business Advocacy Review Panel Requirements, GAO/GGD-98-36, March 18, 1996.

[46] U.S. General Accounting Office, Regulatory Flexibility Act: Inherent Weaknesses May Limit Its Usefulness for Small Governments, GAO/HRD-91-16, January 11, 1991.

[47] U.S. General Accounting Office, Regulatory Flexibility Act: Status of Agencies' Compliance, GAO/GGD-94-105, April 27, 1994.

[48] U.S. General Accounting Office, Regulatory Flexibility Act: Agencies' Interpretations of Review Requirements Vary, GAO/GGD-99-55, April 2, 1999; U.S. General Accounting Office, Regulatory Flexibility Act: Implementation in EPA Program Offices and Proposed Lead Rule, GAO/GGD-00-193. September 20, 2000.

[49] U.S. General Accounting Office, Regulatory Flexibility Act: Key Terms Still Need to Be Clarified, GAO-01-669T, April 24, 2001.

[50] For more information about the RFA, see CRS Report RL34355, The Regulatory Flexibility Act: Implementation Issues and Proposed Reforms, coordinated by Maeve P. Carey.

[51] U.S. General Accounting Office, Regulatory Reform: Compliance Guide Requirement Has Had Little Effect on Agency Practices, GAO-02-172, December 28, 2001.

[52] In 2007, Congress enacted some changes to these requirements. See P.L. 110-28, Title VI, Subtitle B, Section 7005. Among other things, agencies must prepare compliance guides for any rule for which it must prepare a final regulatory flexibility analysis, and must post the guides on their websites.

[53] U.S. General Accounting Office, Regulatory Reform: Implementation of Selected Agencies' Civil Penalty Relief Policies for Small Entities, GAO-01-280, February 20, 2001.

[54] For a detailed discussion of CRA procedures, see CRS Report RL31160, Disapproval of Regulations by Congress: Procedure Under the Congressional Review Act, by Richard S. Beth.

[55] Nevertheless, some rules have not been submitted. See CRS Report R40997, Congressional Review Act: Rules Not Submitted to GAO and Congress, by Curtis W. Copeland.

[56] The CRA defines "major" rules as "any rule that the Administrator of the Office of Information and Regulatory Affairs of the Office of Management and Budget finds has resulted in or is likely to result in—(A) an annual effect on the economy of $100,000,000 or more; (B) a major increase in costs or prices for consumers, individual industries, Federal, State, or local government agencies, or geographic regions; or (C) significant adverse effects on competition, employment, investment, productivity, innovation, or on the ability of United States-based enterprises to compete with foreign-based enterprises in domestic and export markets."

[57] To view these reports, see http://www.gao.gov/decisions/majrule/majrule.php.

[58] See, for example, Susan E. Dudley, "Reversing Midnight Regulations," Regulation, vol. 24 (Spring 2001), p. 9, who noted that the "veto threat is diminished [after a transition], since the president whose administration issued the regulations is no longer in office." For more information about midnight rulemaking generally, see CRS Report R42612, Midnight Rulemaking, by Maeve P. Carey. For a discussion of which rules may be carried over and disapproved after a transition, see CRS Report RL34633, Congressional Review Act: Disapproval of Rules in a Subsequent Session of Congress, by Curtis W. Copeland and Richard S. Beth.

[59] For more information on appropriations limitations, see CRS Report R41634, Limitations in Appropriations Measures: An Overview of Procedural Issues, by Jessica Tollestrup.

[60] For an overview of UMRA, see CRS Report R40957, Unfunded Mandates Reform Act: History, Impact, and Issues, by Robert Jay Dilger and Richard S. Beth.

[61] In recent years, OIRA's annual report on UMRA has been combined with its report on the costs and benefits of federal regulations. See, for example, Office of Management and Budget, Office of Information and Regulatory Affairs, 2012 Report to Congress on the Benefits and Costs of Federal Regulations and Unfunded Mandates on State, Local, and Tribal Entities, available at http://www.whitehouse.gov/sites/default/files/omb/ inforeg/ 2012_cb/ 2012_cost_benefit_report.pdf.

[62] U.S. General Accounting Office, Unfunded Mandates: Reform Act Has Had Little Effect on Agencies' Rulemaking Actions, GAO/GGD-98-30, February 4, 1998.

[63] U.S. General Accounting Office, Unfunded Mandates: Analysis of Reform Act Coverage, GAO-04-637, May 12, 2004.

[64] U.S. Government Accountability Office, Unfunded Mandates: Views Vary About Reform Act's Strengths, Weaknesses, and Options for Improvement, GAO-05-454, March 31, 2005.

[65] Testimony of Denise M. Fantone, Director, Strategic Issues, U.S. Government Accountability Office, before the Subcommittee on Technology, Information Policy, Intergovernmental Relations and Procurement Reform, House Committee on Oversight of Government Management, available at http://www.gao.gov/products/GAO-11-385T.

[66] OMB published those government-wide guidelines in interim form on September 28, 2001, and in updated final form on February 22, 2002. See Office of Management and Budget, "Guidelines for Ensuring and Maximizing the Quality, Objectivity, Utility, and Integrity of Information Disseminated by Federal Agencies; Republication," Federal Register, vol. 67, no. 36, February 22, 2002, p. 8452.

[67] For a copy of this report, see http://www.whitehouse.gov/sites/default/files/omb/inforeg/fy 03_info_quality_rpt.pdf.

[68] The criticisms raised by OMB Watch are available on the Center for Effective Government's website at http://www.foreffectivegov.org/node/2022 and http://www.foreffectivegov.org/ node/2031.

[69] Salt Institute; Chamber of Commerce of the United States of America v. Michael O. Leavitt, Secretary of Health and Human Services, No. 05-1097, March 6, 2006.

[70] In re: Operation of the Missouri River Sys. Litig., No. 03-MD-1555 at 49 (D. Minn. June 21, 2004) (order granting motions for summary judgment); and Salt Institute and the Chamber of Commerce of the United States of America v. Tommy G. Thompson, Secretary, U.S. Department of Health and Human Services, Civil Action No. 04-359, November 15, 2004. In the Salt Institute case, the court ruled that there is no private right of action under the IQA, saying that the "language in the IQA reflects Congress's intent that any challenges to the quality of information disseminated by federal agencies should take place in administrative proceedings before federal agencies and not the courts." The court also said that judicial review under the APA was not available because the agency's actions did not constitute a "final agency action," and because the agency decisions were within the discretion provided to the agency by law.

[71] Office of Management and Budget, Executive Office of the President, "Proposed Bulletin on Peer Review and Information Quality," Federal Register, vol. 68, no. 178, September 15, 2003, p. 54023.

[72] For a copy of the revised peer review bulletin, see http://www.whitehouse.gov/sites/default/files/omb/assets/omb/ inforeg/peer_review041404.pdf. For a summary of the public and agency comments provided regarding the first bulletin, see http://www.whitehouse.gov/sites/default/files/omb/assets/omb/inforeg/peer_review_comment.pdf. Copies of the comments can be viewed at http://www.whitehouse.gov/omb/inforeg_2003iq_iq_list/.

[73] Office of Management and Budget, Final Information Quality Bulletin for Peer Review, December 16, 2004, available at http://www.whitehouse.gov/sites/default/files/omb/assets/omb/memoranda/fy2005/m05-03.pdf.

[74] Office of Management and Budget, Final Information Quality Bulletin for Peer Review, 70 Federal Register 2664 (January 14, 2005).

[75] In a September 20, 2001, memorandum to the President's Management Council, the OIRA Administrator previously indicated that, during its reviews of agencies' draft rules under Executive Order 12866, it would give a "measure of deference" to regulatory analyses that had been peer reviewed.

[76] For more information, see CRS Report RL32680, Peer Review: OMB's Proposed, Revised, and Final Bulletins, by Curtis W. Copeland and Eric A. Fischer.

[77] For more information, see CRS Report R40520, Federal Advisory Committees: An Overview, by Wendy Ginsberg.

[78] For a complete discussion of negotiated rulemaking, see Administrative Conference of the United States, Negotiated Rulemaking Sourcebook (September 1995).

[79] Cary Coglianese, "Assessing Consensus: The Promise and Performance of Negotiated Rulemaking," Duke University Law Journal, vol. 46 (1997), pp. 1255-1349.

[80] Laura I. Langbein and Cornelius M. Kerwin, "Regulatory Negotiation versus Conventional Rulemaking: Claims, Counterclaims, and Empirical Evidence," Journal of Public Administration Research and Theory, vol. 10 (2000), pp. 599-632.

[81] For more information, see CRS Report RL32452, Negotiated Rulemaking, by Curtis W. Copeland. The author of that report has retired from CRS; questions about its content can be directed to Maeve P. Carey.

[82] For a discussion of federal policies relating to certification and consensus standards, see U.S. General Accounting Office, Certification Requirements: New Guidance Should Encourage Transparency in Agency Decisionmaking, GAO/GGD-99-170, September 24, 1999.

[83] The accounting statement requirement had been included in appropriations bills for several previous years on a year-to-year basis.

[84] See http://www.whitehouse.gov/omb/inforeg_regpol_reports_congress/ for a compilation of these reports.

[85] For a comparison of the Regulations.gov website with individual agency systems, see U.S. General Accounting Office, Electronic Rulemaking: Efforts to Facilitate Public Participation Can Be Improved, GAO-03-90, September 17, 2003.

[86] For more information, see CRS Report RL34210, Electronic Rulemaking in the Federal Government, by Curtis W. Copeland. The author of that report has retired from CRS; questions about its content can be directed to Maeve P. Carey.

[87] These lists of compliance assistance resources are available on the OMB website at http://www.whitehouse.gov/omb/inforeg/infocoll.html#sbpra and on the SBA website at http://www.sba.gov/ombudsman/compliance/ complianceassist.html.

[88] Executive Order 12866, "Regulatory Planning and Review," 58 Federal Register 51735, October 4, 1993.

[89] Although issued on September 30, 1993, the executive order was not printed in the Federal Register until several days later.

[90] For a current list of regulations under OIRA review or reviews completed within the past 30 days, see http://www.reginfo.gov/public/.

[91] In January 1996, OIRA published a document that described "best practices" for preparing the economic analyses called for by the executive order. This document was revised and issued as guidance in 2000. In September 2003, OMB and the Council of Economic Advisors finalized new guidance for agencies on regulatory analysis, refining and replacing the 1996 "best practices" document. For a copy of this guidance, see http://www. whitehouse.gov/omb/ circulars_a004_a-4. For more detailed information of the cost-benefit analysis requirements associated with E.O. 12866, as well as other cost-benefit analysis requirements, see CRS Report R41974, Cost-Benefit and Other Analysis Requirements in the Rulemaking Process, by Maeve P. Carey.

[92] OIRA has indicated that it will try and accommodate any request for a meeting with parties outside of the federal government. OIRA discloses these contacts on its website at http://www.whitehouse.gov/omb/oira_meetings/. A representative from the agency issuing the rule must be invited to any such meeting.

[93] Executive Order 13258 reassigned certain responsibilities from the Vice President to the President's chief of staff, but otherwise did not change the OIRA review process. See Executive Order 13258, Amending Executive Order 12866 on Regulatory Planning and Review, Federal Register, vol. 67, no. 40, February 28, 2002, p. 9385.

[94] U.S. General Accounting Office, Rulemaking: OMB's Role in Reviews of Agencies' Draft Rules and the Transparency of Those Reviews, GAO-03-929, September 22, 2003.

[95] U.S. Government Accountability Office, Federal Rulemaking: Improvements Needed to Monitoring and Evaluation of Rules Development as Well as to the Transparency of OMB Regulatory Reviews, GAO-09-205, April 2009. http://www.gao.gov/assets/290/288538.pdf.

[96] U.S. General Accounting Office, Regulatory Reform: Agencies' Efforts to Eliminate and Revise Rules Yield Mixed Results, GAO/GGD-98-3, October 2, 1997.

[97] On the same day that E.O. 13422 was issued, OMB also issued a "Final Bulletin for Agency Good Guidance Practices" that mirrored, in many respects, the provisions in this section of the executive order. Unlike the order, however, the bulletin requires agencies to include certain standard elements in their significant guidance documents, to list those documents on the agencies' websites, and to publish a notice in the Federal Register soliciting public

comments on economically significant documents. To view a copy of this bulletin, see http://www.whitehouse.gov/ omb/memoranda/fy2007/m07-07.pdf; and Office of Management and Budget, "Final Bulletin for Agency Good Guidance Practices," 72 Federal Register 3432, January 25, 2007.

[98] Executive Order 13497, "Revocation of Certain Executive Orders Concerning Regulatory Planning and Review," 74 Federal Register 6113, February 4, 2009.

[99] Executive Order 13563, "Improving Regulation and Regulatory Review," 76 Federal Register 3821, January 21, 2011.

[100] Agency retrospective review plans can be viewed at http://exchange.regulations.gov/topic/eo-13563.

[101] See http://www.whitehouse.gov/sites/default/files/omb/memoranda/2011/m11-10.pdf.

[102] Executive Order 13579, "Regulation and Independent Regulatory Agencies," 76 Federal Register 41587, July 11, 2011.

[103] Executive Order 13132, "Federalism," 64 Federal Register 43255, August 10, 1999.

[104] Executive Order 12612, the previous executive order on federalism, also gave federal agencies broad discretion to determine the applicability of its requirements. GAO examined the implementation of this order and concluded that its analytical requirements were rarely implemented. See U.S. General Accounting Office, Federalism: Previous Initiatives Have Had Little Effect on Agency Rulemaking, GAO/T-GGD-99-3, June 30, 1999.

[105] Executive Order 12630, "Governmental Actions and Interference with Constitutionally Protected Property Rights," 53 Federal Register 8859, March 18, 1988.

[106] For an analysis of how this executive order has been implemented, see U.S. General Accounting Office, Regulatory Takings: Implementation of Executive Order on Government Actions Affecting Private Property Use, GAO-03-1015, September 19, 2003.

[107] Executive Order 12889, "Implementation of the North American Free Trade Agreement," 58 Federal Register 69681, December 30, 1993.

[108] Executive Order 12898, "Federal Actions to Address Environmental Justice in Minority Populations and Low-Income Populations," 59 Federal Register 7629, February 16, 1994.

[109] Executive Order 12988, "Civil Justice Reform," 61 Federal Register 4729, February 7, 1996.

[110] Executive Order 13045, "Protection of Children from Environmental Health Risks and Safety Risks," 62 Federal Register 19885, April 23, 1997.

[111] Executive Order 13175, "Consultation and Coordination with Indian Tribal Governments," 65 Federal Register 67249, November 9, 2000.

[112] Executive Order 13211, "Actions Concerning Regulations That Significantly Affect Energy Supply, Distribution, or Use," 66 Federal Register 28355, May 22, 2001.

[113] Executive Order 13272, "Proper Consideration of Small Entities in Agency Rulemaking," 67 Federal Register 53461, August 16, 2002.

[114] Executive Order 13609, "Promoting International Regulatory Cooperation," 77 Federal Register 26413, May 1, 2012.

[115] Executive Order 13610, "Identifying and Reducing Regulatory Burdens," 77 Federal Register 28469, May 14, 2012.

[116] Administrative Conference of the U.S., "Improving the Environment for Agency Rulemaking," 59 Federal Register 4670, February 1, 1994.

In: Federal Rulemaking
Editor: Norman A. Elwin
ISBN: 978-1-63463-724-4

Chapter 2

FEDERAL RULEMAKING: AGENCIES INCLUDED KEY ELEMENTS OF COST-BENEFIT ANALYSIS, BUT EXPLANATIONS OF REGULATIONS' SIGNIFICANCE COULD BE MORE TRANSPARENT*

United States Government Accountability Office

WHY GAO DID THIS STUDY

Federal agencies issue thousands of regulations each year to achieve national goals. For the few hundred of these rules deemed to be significant, agencies are required to assess expected costs and benefits. For the subset of these rules estimated to have the greatest economic impact, agencies must also include an assessment of alternatives.

GAO was asked to review agencies' compliance with broadly applicable directives and guidance related to significant federal rulemaking. This report addresses (1) how often and to what extent significant, economically significant, and major rules include key elements for assessing or analyzing benefits and costs; and (2) how and to what extent agencies assess the quality of the scientific, technical, and other types of data they use to consider benefits

* This is an edited, reformatted and augmented version of the United States Government Accountability Office publication, GAO-14-714, dated September 2014.

and costs. To answer these objectives, GAO reviewed a generalizable sample of 109 significant and 57 economically significant rules issued by executive agencies and all 37 major rules issued by independent agencies and published in the *Federal Register* from July 1, 2011, to June 30, 2013. GAO also conducted roundtable discussions with the 17 executive and independent agencies with the largest number of rules in GAO's sample.

WHAT GAO RECOMMENDS

To improve the transparency of the rulemaking process, GAO recommends the Office of Management and Budget (OMB) work with agencies to clearly communicate why certain rules are designated as significant. OMB staff did not state whether they agreed or disagreed with the recommendation.

WHAT GAO FOUND

How often and to what extent agencies included selected key elements of cost- benefit analysis varied by rule type. The selected key elements in GAO's review are a statement of purpose; monetized or quantified costs and benefits or a qualitative discussion of them; and a discussion of alternatives. The 203 rules GAO reviewed are categorized into three broad, nonmutually exclusive categories—major, economically significant, and significant rules—based in part on their likely economic effects. Between July 1, 2011, and June 30, 2013, agencies included the selected key elements in the majority of the economically significant and major rules and less often in significant rules. Agencies sometimes included these key elements even when they may not have been required to do so. The results of GAO's review of agencies' regulatory cost- benefit analyses for these rules are as follows:

Statement of purpose: A statement of purpose provides the underlying reason for the rule. Agencies included this element in all rules.

Costs and benefits: Monetizing costs and benefits allows decision makers to evaluate different regulatory options using a common measure. Agencies included a mix of monetized and quantified costs and benefits and qualitative discussions of costs and benefits in most economically significant and major rules, but less often in significant rules. Almost all economically significant rules contained some monetized costs, as did most major rules and some significant rules. Many agency officials said they try to monetize costs and benefits whenever possible, regardless of rule type; however, monetizing benefits can be more difficult than monetizing costs. For example, officials said it is challenging to estimate the value of enhancing national security. Agency officials said that obtaining sufficient or quality data is a primary challenge to cost-benefit analysis.

Alternatives: Analyzing alternatives helps agencies to decide on the best regulatory approach. Agencies identified alternatives in most economically significant and major rules and in some significant rules. Agencies said they sometimes do not identify alternatives because the statute requiring the rule is so specific that considering alternatives is not a practical use of resources.

Agencies included a discussion of how they assessed the data quality more often in economically significant rules than in significant or major rules. Agencies used various methods to assess the data, depending on the type and use of the data. For example, agencies used the peer review process to help ensure science- driven data were the most current and appropriate data available. Only three of the seventeen agencies that participated in GAO's roundtables reported reevaluating cost-benefit analyses once a rule had been issued.

GAO's review also found that for the majority of the 109 significant rules reviewed, the rulemaking process is not as transparent as it could be. This is because 72 percent of these rules included no language to explain why the rule was designated as significant. Some agency officials indicated that the Office of Management and Budget's Office of Information and Regulatory Affairs did not always provide a reason for changing a rule's designation to significant. The rulemaking process could be more transparent if significance designations were explained and communicated.

ABBREVIATIONS

APA	Administrative Procedure Act
CRA	Congressional Review Act
EPA	Environmental Protection Agency
FAR	Federal Acquisition Regulation
GSA	General Services Administration
NLRB	National Labor Relations Board

NRC	Nuclear Regulatory Commission
OIRA	Office of Information and Regulatory Affairs
OMB	Office of Management and Budget
PRA	Paperwork Reduction Act
RFA	Regulatory Flexibility Act
UMRA	Unfunded Mandates Reform Act
WTO GPA	World Trade Organization Government Procurement Agreement

* * *

September 11, 2014

The Honorable Ron Johnson
Ranking Member
Subcommittee on Financial and Contracting Oversight
Committee on Homeland Security and Governmental Affairs
United States Senate

The Honorable Mark R. Warner
Chairman
Task Force on Government Performance
Committee on the Budget
United States Senate

Federal regulations are one of the many tools that agencies use to achieve national goals, such as improving the economy and protecting the health and safety of the public and the environment.[1] While regulations can generate substantial benefits to society, they also have costs. The Office of Management and Budget (OMB) estimated annual benefits from major federal regulations issued in fiscal years 2003 through 2012 to be $193 billion to $800 billion and estimated annual costs of $57 billion to $84 billion.[2] For more than two decades, presidents have issued a number of executive orders directing agencies to analyze the costs and benefits of regulations in order to anticipate and evaluate the likely consequences of rules. OMB's Office of Information and Regulatory Affairs (OIRA) is responsible for ensuring federal regulations issued by agencies, other than independent regulatory agencies, follow executive order requirements for regulatory analysis, including analyzing costs and benefits.[3] The regulatory philosophy and principles of these executive orders recognize that in deciding whether and how to regulate, agencies should assess all costs and benefits of available regulatory alternatives, including the alternative of not regulating.

Executive agencies promulgate thousands of rules each year. In most years, agencies are required to submit only a few hundred of these rules to OIRA for review—only those OIRA has determined are "significant regulatory actions."[4] For these rules, agencies are required to provide OIRA with an assessment of costs and benefits. For a portion of these rules—those with the largest expected economic effects (approximately 17 percent for fiscal years 2003 through 2012)—agencies are required to submit a more detailed analysis of costs and benefits to OIRA, including an analysis of potential alternative regulatory actions.[5] Independent regulatory agencies' rules are not subject to OIRA review, but may have annual economic effects in the hundreds of millions of dollars. A large body of academic and economic research exists on the regulatory analyses (and their cost-benefit analyses) performed on executive agency rules with the largest economic effects. Less is known about rules with smaller economic effects, even though in the aggregate their economic impact can be large.

You asked us to review agencies' compliance with broadly applicable directives and guidance related to significant federal rulemaking. This report addresses (1) how often and to what extent significant rules (including economically significant rules) issued by executive agencies, and major rules issued by independent regulatory agencies, contain key elements for assessing or analyzing benefits and costs; and (2) how and to what extent agencies assess the quality of the scientific, technical, and other types of data they use to consider costs and benefits.

To answer our first objective, we reviewed 203 final rules that were issued and published in the *Federal Register* between July 1, 2011 and June 30, 2013 to determine whether they contained what we consider (for the purposes of this report) key elements of a cost-benefit analysis: a discussion of the problem the rule intends to address; monetized, quantified, or qualitatively discussed costs; monetized, quantified, or qualitatively discussed benefits; and a discussion of alternatives.[6] These four broad elements stem from several sources including Executive Orders 12866 and 13563, OMB's *Circular A-4,* and general economic principles.[7] *Circular A-4*, consistent with standard economic principles, identifies these selected elements as basic elements to include in the regulatory analysis required by the executive orders.[8] Although other elements could be viewed as key to include in a full and complete regulatory analysis, we focused our review on these selected elements because they are considered to be basic elements important to any regulatory cost-benefit assessment and analysis. We recognize that agencies were not required to include all of the key elements for all of the rule types we reviewed and that it may not always be feasible to include all key elements in a rule. Further, our analysis was not designed to evaluate the quality of the cost-benefit analysis in the rules. The presence of all key elements does not provide information regarding the quality of the analysis, nor does the absence of a key element necessarily imply a deficiency in a cost-benefit analysis.

Although rules may fall into multiple categories—such as being both economically significant and major—we divided our analysis into three distinct categories: economically significant, significant, and major. For the purposes of this report, we include economically significant rules in our sample separately from significant rules. While executive agency rules can be major, in our sample for this report, they were also all economically significant. In this report, we use the term major rules to mean only those major rules issued by independent regulatory agencies. For significant and economically significant rules, we reviewed a stratified random sample drawn from the full population of final rules of both types issued between July 1, 2011 and June 30, 2013. We reviewed 109 significant rules and 57 economically significant rules. Estimates of these populations are based on these sample data and are subject to sampling error.[9] We also reviewed the population of all 37 major rules issued by independent regulatory agencies within the same time frame. Values reported for those rules are not subject to sampling error and are not estimates but population values.

To supplement the rule review and to answer our second objective, we conducted roundtable discussions with 17 of the 32 independent regulatory and executive agencies that issued the rules we reviewed.[10] At these roundtables, we asked the agency officials involved in the development of agency regulations to discuss their interactions with OIRA, the challenges they face in including the select key elements of cost-benefit analyses, the steps they take to assess the quality of their data, and how often (if at all) they compare estimated costs and benefits in rules to outcome data after rules are implemented. At the executive agency roundtables, we asked agency officials to compare their approaches to cost-benefit analyses in significant and economically significant rules. Further information about our rule review sample and roundtables can be found in appendix I.

We conducted this performance audit from June 2013 to September 2014 in accordance with generally accepted government auditing standards. Those standards require that we plan and perform the audit to obtain sufficient, appropriate evidence to provide a reasonable basis for our findings and conclusions based on our audit objectives. We believe that the evidence obtained provides a reasonable basis for our findings and conclusions based on our audit objectives.

BACKGROUND

The Paperwork Reduction Act of 1980 (PRA) established OIRA as an office within OMB.[11] OIRA is responsible for the coordinated review of executive agency rulemakings to ensure that regulations are consistent with applicable laws, the President's priorities, and the principles set forth in executive orders. Agencies provide OIRA with basic summary information when drafting rules to determine if additional OIRA review is required. If so, agencies provide any required analyses (including information on estimated costs and benefits) to OIRA before issuing a final rule. OIRA desk officers review the rule and related documents and may request changes or additional analyses. Further, OIRA is responsible for ensuring that decisions made by one agency do not conflict with the policies or actions taken or planned by another agency.

OMB also provides guidance to agencies on the development of regulatory analysis, of which cost-benefit analysis is a primary tool. According to Executive Order 12866, OIRA is to be the repository of expertise concerning regulatory issues. OIRA is also responsible under PRA for reviewing all information collections by the federal government.[12] Independent regulatory agencies are not subject to OIRA regulatory review, although OIRA does interact with these agencies on other regulatory matters, such as approving information collections and making major rule determinations.

Several laws, executive orders, and OMB guidance provide direction for agencies in the rulemaking process and impose requirements on agencies, depending on the type of rule being promulgated.[13] These laws and executive orders also define four broad categories of rules. These categories—which are not necessarily mutually exclusive—are major, significant, economically significant, and non-major/non-significant.

Major rules are defined by the Congressional Review Act (CRA).[14] CRA applies to both executive and independent regulatory agencies. Major rules are those that will likely result in

- an annual effect on the economy of $100 million or more, or
- major increases in costs or prices for consumers, individual industries, federal, state, or local government agencies, or geographic regions, or
- significant adverse effects on competition, employment, investment, productivity, or innovation, or on the ability of United States-based enterprises to compete with foreign-based enterprises in domestic and export markets.

Under CRA, OIRA is responsible for making major rule designations for both executive and independent regulatory agencies.[15] Rules that are not designated as major are referred to as non-major.

Significant and economically significant rules are defined in Executive Order 12866 for executive agencies. In addition to being major or non- major, executive agency rules are also identified as significant, economically significant, or non-significant regulatory actions under Executive Order 12866. According to OMB, the majority of rules issued every year by executive agencies are not significant regulatory actions. These regulatory actions may include rules that affect a small number of individuals or entities or only affect agency operations.[16]

A rule is significant under Executive Order 12866 if it meets one of the following four criteria:

- The rule is likely to have an annual effect on the economy of $100 million or more or adversely affect in a material way the economy, a sector of the economy, productivity, competition, jobs, the environment, public health or safety, or state, local, or tribal governments or communities.
- The rule is likely to create a serious inconsistency or otherwise interfere with an action taken or planned by another agency.
- The rule is likely to materially alter the budgetary impact of entitlements, grants, user fees, or loan programs or the rights and obligations of recipients thereof.
- The rule is likely to raise novel legal or policy issues arising out of legal mandates, the President's priorities, or the principles set forth in Executive Order 12866.

Economically significant rules, a subset of significant rules, are those that meet the first criteria above for significant rules. The definition of economically significant is largely similar to the definition of major rules.[17]

Only executive agency rules can be classified as economically significant, but both executive agencies and independent regulatory agencies can issue major rules. Generally, economically significant rules issued by executive agencies are also classified as major rules. Figure 1 shows the relationship between significant and economically significant rules for executive agencies.

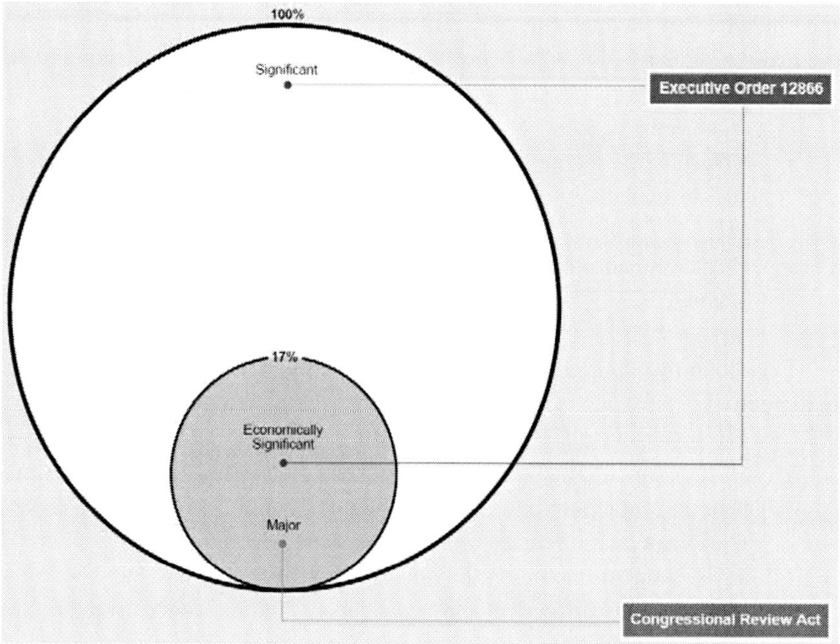

Source: GAO analysis of Executive Order 12866 and the Congressional Review Act. | GAO-14-714.

Note: This figure reflects rules issued only by executive agencies and does not include major rules issued by independent regulatory agencies. During fiscal years 2003 through 2012, approximately 17 percent of the significant regulations issued by executive agencies were also considered economically significant or major.

Figure 1. Rule Type Definitions for Executive Agency Rules.
(See Appendix IV for additional information regarding Figure 1.)

Requirements for Regulatory Analysis and Oversight

Executive Order 12866 promotes a regulatory philosophy and set of principles that, to the extent permitted by law and where applicable, encourages agencies to assess costs, benefits, and available regulatory alternatives in all rules, including the alternative of not regulating. Executive Order 13563 reaffirms this philosophy and these principles.[18] These executive orders include more specific requirements for some agencies and some rules. Executive agencies are required to include certain information about the costs and benefits of significant and economically significant rules in final rulemaking dockets. For significant rules, executive agencies are required to include

- a reasonably detailed description of the need for the regulatory action and an explanation of how the regulatory action will meet that need, and
- an assessment of the potential costs and benefits of the regulatory action.[19]

For economically significant rules, executive agencies are further required to include

- an assessment, including the underlying analysis, of the costs and benefits anticipated from the regulatory action, with, to the extent feasible, a quantification of those costs and benefits; and
- an assessment, including the underlying analysis, of costs and benefits of potentially effective and reasonably feasible alternatives to the planned regulation, as well as an explanation of why the planned regulatory action is preferable to the identified alternatives.[20]

According to OMB guidance, agencies should consider a range of potentially effective and reasonably feasible regulatory alternatives when analyzing alternatives. The relevant alternatives might involve different approaches, with distinct advantages and disadvantages, and may include the option of not regulating, among other options. Agencies can also analyze alternatives with varying enforcement methods, stringency requirements, compliance dates, or requirements based on firm size or geographic location.

Independent regulatory agencies are not subject to Executive Order 12866 requirements. However, these independent regulatory agencies, as well as executive agencies, may be subject to other statutory provisions that require the agencies to include certain types of analyses in rules, including costs and benefits. For example, all agencies, including independent regulatory agencies, must meet the requirements of PRA,[21] the Regulatory Flexibility Act (RFA) (impact on small entities),[22] and executive agencies must meet the requirements of the Unfunded Mandates Reform Act (UMRA) in certain circumstances.[23] In addition, executive and independent regulatory agencies may have agency-specific statutory requirements for assessing or analyzing costs, benefits, or alternatives.[24] Table 1 summarizes definitions of rule types and select requirements for regulatory analysis.

Circular A-4 was issued by OMB in 2003 to provide guidance and best practices to federal agencies on conducting regulatory analyses.[25] Cost- benefit analysis, the primary tool of regulatory analysis, can provide government agencies, Congress, and the public with important information about the potential effects of new regulations.[26] *Circular A-4* offers a framework for how agencies can analyze the costs and benefits of a proposed regulation, but generally does not prescribe the specific assumptions or values to use in analyzing the potential effects of rules. This flexibility is intended to allow agencies to apply the framework to their particular regulations and regulated entities. According to *Circular A-4*, a good regulatory analysis should include three basic elements: a statement of the need for the proposed action; an examination of alternative approaches; and an evaluation of the benefits and costs (quantitative and qualitative) of the proposed action and the main alternatives identified by the analysis. OIRA uses *Circular A-4* as the primary guidance in reviewing regulatory analyses. Figure 2 shows how OIRA's review and requirements for regulatory analyses differ based on the type of agency and rule.

As shown in figure 2, one step in regulatory analysis is for an agency to determine if a rule is a major rule under the CRA, a significant regulatory action under Executive Order 12866, or both. Under CRA, OIRA is responsible for determining if rules are major for all agencies, including independent regulatory agencies. Executive agencies must also determine if their rules are significant regulatory actions, including determining whether the rules are economically significant and OIRA must concur. OIRA determines if independent regulatory agencies' rules are major before the rules are issued.[27]

Table 1. Summary of Selected Definitions and Requirements of Executive Order 12866 and the Congressional Review Act

	Significant rules[a]	Economically significant rules	Major rules
Defined by	Executive Order 12866	Executive Order 12866	Congressional Review Act
Definition	Likely to • interfere with another agency's actions, • materially alter the budgetary impact of entitlements, grants, user fees, or loan programs or the rights and obligations of recipients thereof, or • raise novel legal or policy issues.	Likely to • have an annual effect on the economy of $100 million or more, or • adversely affect the economy, productivity, competition, jobs, the environment, public health or safety, or state, local, or tribal governments or communities.	Likely to • have an annual effect on the economy of $100 million or more, • cause major increases in costs or prices, or • have significant adverse effects on competition, employment, investment, productivity, or innovation.
Definition applies to	Executive agencies	Executive agencies	Executive and independent regulatory agencies
Cost-benefit analysis requirements	Executive Order 12866 directs agencies issuing rules that meet the criteria of significant regulatory actions to • describe the need for the action and explain how the action will meet that need, and • assess potential costs and benefits of the regulatory action. Significant rules may be subject to additional statutory requirements for assessing costs, benefits, or alternatives that may not apply to every rule.	In addition to the requirements for significant rules, Executive Order 12866 directs agencies issuing rules that meet the criteria of economically significant regulatory actions to also • quantify costs and benefits when feasible, and • assess costs and benefits of feasible alternatives and explain why the planned action is preferable to the alternative. Economically significant rules may be subject to additional statutory requirements for assessing costs, benefits, or alternatives that may not apply to every rule.	In addition to the requirements for executive agencies in Executive Order 12866, major rules issued by executive and independent regulatory agencies may be subject to statutory requirements for assessing costs, benefits, or alternatives. The Congressional Review Act requires executive and independent regulatory agencies to submit any cost-benefit analyses to the Congress and GAO.

Source: GAO analysis of Executive Order 12866 and the Congressional Review Act. | GAO-14-714

Note:

[a] Economically significant rules are a subset of significant rules. For the purposes of this table, significant rules exclude the subset of economically significant rules, which is defined and discussed separately.

AGENCIES INCLUDED KEY ELEMENTS OF COST-BENEFIT ANALYSIS IN THE MAJORITY OF ECONOMICALLY SIGNIFICANT AND MAJOR RULES AND IN ABOUT HALF OF SIGNIFICANT RULES, BUT INFORMATION ON RULE DESIGNATION LACKED TRANSPARENCY

Agencies and OIRA Are Not Always Transparent about How Rules Are Designated

OIRA staff told us that executive agencies typically make a preliminary assessment of a rule's designation as significant or not when planning their regulatory actions.[28] The 109 significant (excluding economically significant) rules we reviewed ranged from those implementing minor, low-cost technical changes to those with economic effects just under the (economically significant) $100 million threshold; these rules generally contained a section describing the actions taken by the agency to fulfill regulatory requirements and a statement of whether the rule was a significant regulatory action or not. However, 72 percent of these significant rules lacked specific language to explain why they were designated as significant. Agencies did not include this information when drafting the rules, and OIRA did not require it to be included when they reviewed the rules.[29] A few agencies told us that they did not always have the reason for the significance determination from OIRA.

OIRA staff told us that OIRA usually agrees with agency determinations about a rule's significance and that OIRA staff generally discuss the basis for their significance determinations with agency officials. However, agency officials said that OIRA has at times changed the agencies' designation of some rules from non-significant to significant and that OIRA does not always provide a reason when it does so. Agency officials said that when OIRA does not tell them the reason why the rules are designated as significant, some officials assume the reason for a changed designation could be due to OIRA's consideration of the rule as "likely to raise novel legal or policy issues," one of the four categories of significant rules.[30] (One agency's officials said it was to ensure the rule is circulated to other agencies for comment.)

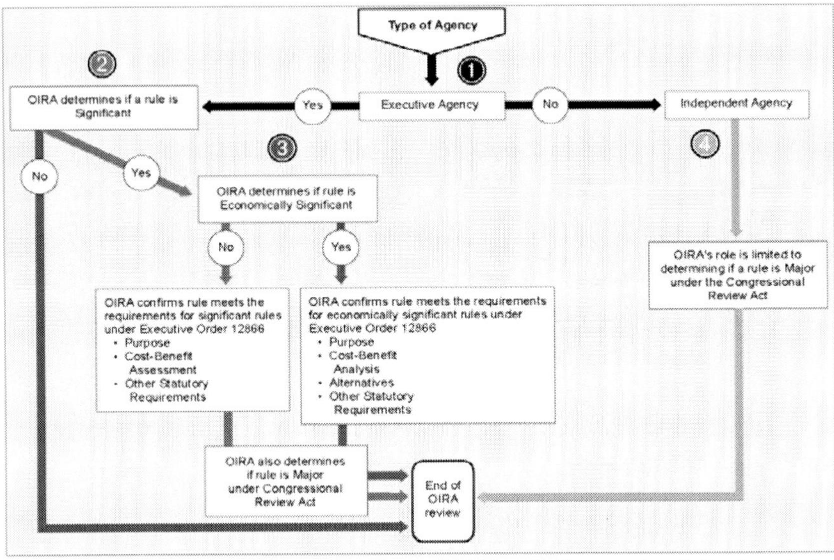

Source: GAO analysis of Executive Order 12866 and Congressional Review Act. | GAO-14-714

Note: Criteria and requirements for significant and economically significant rules are derived from Exec. Order Nos. 12866 and 13563. Criteria for major rules are derived from the Congressional Review Act.

Figure 2. Office of Information and Regulatory Affairs (OIRA) Review Process for Significant, Economically Significant, and Major Rules under Executive Order 12866 and the Congressional Review Act.

Officials from some executive agencies told us that recently OIRA has more frequently changed the designation of rules. Some agency officials said that changes in rule designation can vary by agency or by OIRA desk officer (the staff at OIRA who review agency rule designations). For example, officials from one agency told us that OIRA changes the designation of its agency's rules about 50 percent of the time, while officials from another agency said OIRA rarely disagreed with their agency's initial designation. OIRA staff told us that there can be variation across agencies because agencies vary in the types of regulations they issue and the desk officers assigned to each agency have discretion to determine how OMB requirements apply to a rule. One of Executive Order 12866's objectives is to make the regulatory process more accessible and open to the public; however, a lack of consistent information explaining why a rule is designated as significant prevents policymakers and the public from knowing how OIRA is applying criteria for